William Bell Scott

Poems, Ballads, Studies From Nature, Sonnets

William Bell Scott

Poems, Ballads, Studies From Nature, Sonnets

ISBN/EAN: 9783744712460

Printed in Europe, USA, Canada, Australia, Japan

Cover: Foto ©Thomas Meinert / pixelio.de

More available books at **www.hansebooks.com**

POEMS

BY

WILLIAM BELL SCOTT.

BALLADS, STUDIES FROM NATURE, SONNETS, ETC.

ILLUSTRATED BY SEVENTEEN ETCHINGS

BY THE AUTHOR AND L. ALMA TADEMA

LONDON
LONGMANS, GREEN, AND CO.
1875

All rights reserved

PREFACE.

EXCEPTING some of the Ballads at the beginning of the volume, and a number of the Sonnets, particularly those called 'The Old Scotch House,' the poems now published have been written many years. This being the case, the author thinks he may indulge in the old-fashioned luxury of a Preface; only a short one, however, and merely to state certain circumstances relating to some of the pieces.

In the present volume the writer has collected together the productions he wishes most to preserve, or at least the majority of these; he has carefully revised them, and lovingly decorated them, with the assistance of a friend, as a duty to himself, and to place before the public in a permanent form his credentials to be considered a poet. For a number of years he has been urged to do something of this kind by friends whose judgment in matters poetic is not mere opinion: sweet is praise from the receivers of praise; and he has been contented without any appeal to the public. But there is a day for all things, and after a period of active work of very various kinds, obeying the maxim, 'What thy hand findeth to do, do it with all thy might,' he thinks the time has come for the pleasant task of putting his poetical house in order.

A number of the following poems have indeed been various times printed before, although never very accessibly to the public. Many of these he has freely revised, believing that the best word is not found even within the Horatian period sometimes, or at least that it depends on the nature of the man whether his first or last thought is the best. He has also restored one or two to their original MS. form. The rhapsody 'To the Memory of P. B. Shelley' first appeared in 'Tait's Edinburgh Magazine' forty-two years ago, and the point of view taken by a student of that day adds some historical interest to the poem, warranting its reproduction here. Shelley's too-easily-uttered metaphysics, and jejune theories, political and moral, derived from and representative of the great French revolution with its three watchwords continually outraged, will never again be lauded in exactly the same manner. Two other pieces towards the end of this volume, 'The Incantation of Hervor,' and 'The Dance of Death,' were produced a year or two later in a little *brochure* called 'The Edinburgh University Souvenir.' The latter poem has been revised. Others not given under the heading 'Juvenile Poems' are equally ancient. One of these, 'Anthony,' although first published in the 'Fortnightly' only a few years ago, is old enough to have been read in a somewhat longer form in MS. by John Wilson. The author remembers the amusement expressed on the lion-like face of that genial literary partizan at the lines near the close of the poem, describing the beggar who tried to strike the charitable with his crutch, finding in them a vivid picture of Christopher North!

Many others have appeared before in a small volume called 'Poems by a Painter,' printed at a provincial press in a careless manner. This title was afterwards appropriated by Sir J. Noel Paton, a painter of sufficient power and invention to exonerate him from intentional transfer. That now called 'The Music of the Spheres,' first saw the light in a very small volume in 1838 under the name of 'Hades,' so that the resemblance that has been supposed to exist between it and the Roman Catholic production of

Dr. Newman called 'The Dream of Gerontius' is accidental as far as the author knows. Other cases wherein a resemblance, either in motive or form, may be fancied to exist to any more modern work, it is not necessary to mention. Originality the writer takes some credit for; he has, moreover, left out some poems whose subjects or motives have been adopted by later poets, and realised in a more poetical or completer manner, considering that the best, not the first, should stand alone.

This concerns rather the author himself than his readers. No external or adventitious merits, nor even purely intellectual qualities, can altogether determine the value of poetry. It must affect us like music or wine, but it must certainly have Wisdom, like an instinct, directing it from within. Every excellent poetic work has a physiognomy of its own, an organic character of its own, the possession or non-possession of which the world will sooner or later sympathetically determine. So fully aware is he of this, and so careless of immediate recognition has he been, that his earlier publications were issued in a way rather fitted to his convenience than to invite attention, and he never once asked their publishers or quasi-publishers for any account of results. The chances of sale for new poetical aspirants out of London were then very small indeed. His former little volumes are, however, entirely unprocurable, he believes.

With regard to the illustrations, the author-and-artist-in-one has given rather pictorial analogues to the sentiment and meaning of the poems than direct representations. He has also to acknowledge the kind aid of one of the most able painters of the age. The artist by natural endowment finds little difficulty, whatever instrument may be placed in his hand; and the writer's friend, L. Alma Tadema, expressed himself at once with the etching-point as if he had used it all his life.

CONTENTS.

	PAGE
LADY JANET, MAY JEAN	1
KRIEMHILD'S TRYST .	7
WOODSTOCK MAZE .	23
THE WITCHES' BALLAD	29
SAINT MARGARET .	35

CONTENTS.

	PAGE
THE RENDEZVOUS	37
'I GO TO BE CURED AT AVILION'	42
ANTHONY	44
LOVE'S CALENDAR	60
A BRIDAL RACE	62
PARTING AND MEETING AGAIN (a Song)	64
LOVE	65

SONNETS.

OUTSIDE THE TEMPLE	73
PARTED LOVE	90

THE OLD SCOTCH HOUSE.

PART I.	97
PART II.	105

STUDIES FROM NATURE.

SUNDAY MORNING ALONE	113
GREEN CHERRIES	118
YOUTH AND AGE	122
AN ARTIST'S BIRTHPLACE	123
MORNING SLEEP	127
MONODY	131
THE DUKE'S FUNERAL	134
MIDNIGHT (written 1831)	138
THE SEASHORE. I. MIST	142
,, ,, II. SUNSHINE	143
REQUIEM	145
THE VENERABLE BEDE IN THE NINETEENTH CENTURY	147

MISCELLANEOUS POEMS.

	PAGE
THE SPHINX	159
A DEDICATION	166
RHYME OF THE SUN-DIAL	169
IN THE VALLEY	171
MAY	173

SONNETS ON LITERARY SUBJECTS.

ON THE INSCRIPTION, KEATS'S GRAVESTONE, ROME	179
WORDSWORTH. I.	180
,, II.	181
,, III.	182
TO THE ARTISTS CALLED P.R.B. (1851)	183
ON CERTAIN CRITICS, &c.	184
EPITAPH OF HUBERT VAN EYCK	185
FRAGMENT OF A SONNET BY RAPHAEL	186
THE MUSICIAN	187
TO MY BROTHER, ON PUBLISHING HIS 'MEMOIR'	188
INSCRIPTION ON ALBERT DÜRER'S GRAVE	189

OCCASIONAL SONNETS.

PYGMALION	193
THE SWAN	194
SPRING LOVE	195
AN ANNIVERSARY	196
THE MIDNIGHT CITY	197
KISSES. I.	198
,, II.	199
THE TRAVELLER LOST	200
THE NIGHTINGALE UNHEARD	201
IN ROME, A.D. 150 (for a Picture)	202

CONTENTS.

	PAGE
COMING AND GOING	203
MY MOTHER. I.	204
,, II.	205
ASSISTANCE DELAYED	206
UNWORTHY AMBITION	207
THE MUSIC OF THE SPHERES	208

JUVENILE POEMS.

TO THE MEMORY OF P. B. SHELLEY	221
TO THE MEMORY OF JOHN KEATS	226
THE INCANTATION OF HERVOR	231
FOUR ACTS OF ST. CUTHBERT	237
THE DANCE OF DEATH	253
A FABLE	263
DEDICATIO POSTICA	271

LIST OF ILLUSTRATIONS.

LOVE ORIGINATING ART	*W. B. Scott.*	*Title-page*
AN OLD CHEST	,,	*p.* xi
LADY JANET	*L. Alma Tadema.*	1
ERIC AND THE WATER-WITCH	,,	7
FAIR ROSAMUND	,,	23
PAX VOBISCUM: A SATIRE (designed by D. Scott)	*W. B. Scott*	44
THE WAY OF LIFE. WHITHER?	,,	71
PENKILL, AYRSHIRE	,,	95
THE GARDEN, PENKILL	,,	105
A STUDY FROM NATURE	,,	111
DESIGN REMEMBERED FROM A DREAM (from a sketch done on waking October 28, 1846)	,,	131
THE GREAT SPHINX	*L. Alma Tadema.*	159
KEATS' GRAVE, ROME	*W. B. Scott*	177
PYGMALION	,,	191
RECREATING GENII	,,	208
THE AUTHOR ÆT. 20 (painted by D. Scott)	,,	219
HERVOR (painted by Alice Boyd, Penkill)	,,	231

LADY JANET, MAY JEAN.

'TWEEN sleeping and waking, 'tween fever and fear,
    The lady Janet, May Jean,
  Felt her mothering hour draw near;
So wearily dreaming 'tween fever and fear;
    The shards have cut the shoeless feet.

May Jean she was with the snood on her head,
Lady Janet she would be were she wed,
But she locked herself in on her lonely bed.
  The housel is borne along the street.

Was it the wise-woman on the bower-stair
    From lady Janet, May Jean?
Wrapt in her thin arms what doth she bear
Against her hard bosom; why speeds she and where
  The wind is about in the crow's nest.

It was the wise-woman no one knew
Came down as the dark night mottled grew,
And, groping her way, to the postern flew.
  The stream doth every cranny quest.

To shoot back the bar and make no sound,
    O lady Janet, May Jean!
She laid down the fardel on the ground,
And the in-rushing cold wind swept all round;—
  Long willow leaves are white below.

But the house dog's near, his scent is keen,
The fardel and wise-wife he ran between,
He snatched and ran and was no more seen.
  Black are the berries of nightshade and sloe.

On the carven bed in the lighted bower
    Turned lady Janet, May Jean,
Waiting it seemed to her, hour on hour,
Hearing the wind creak the vane on the tower;—
  The tide-wave breathes by sink and swell.

Why is she watching with eye and ear,
Shadowed and restless in fever and fear,
When the bolt is drawn and no one near?
Sees she or hears she anything
Except the lamp's flame and the moth's wing?
  Sea-foam seethes the empty shell.

Yes, yes, she hears now a small faint cry,
  Hears lady Janet, May Jean;
She sees on the hearth the fardel lie,
And the shaggy-limbed house dog standing by;—
  The brain swims when the hot winds blow.

Her fair-tressed weak head she lifted then,
And she cried, 'I am lost, oh, never again
Shall I know peace or be honoured of men!'
  The bare breast shrinks beneath the snow.

Her fair hair swept the bolster white,
  The lady Janet's, May Jean's;
And faintly she called, 'Old witch of the night,
You have played me false, you've deceived me quite!'
  The way to hell's by stepping-stones.

At once that wise-woman no one knew
Out of the carven bedstead grew;
Like a real thing came she clear to view.
  The raven is over the dead lamb's bones.

'The dog he followed me as I ran,
  My lady Janet, May Jean,
And snatched it and stole it when I began

To gather the dry leaves and finish our plan;'—
 The eyes of the dying shine I know.
'But hide it again, thou leman of Night,
Wise-woman, witch-woman, make me right;
Hide it in safety before daylight!'
 The warning cock three times will crow.

They are gone, that wise-woman has the power;
 And lady Janet, May Jean,
Again is alone in that lone bower,
Her whole soul listening beyond the tower;—
 The dead are safe i' their graves we say.
Why is her life in her eye and ear,
Writhing and striving in fever and fear,
When the bolt is drawn and no one near?
Sees she or hears she anything
Saving the lamp and the moth's quick wing?
 They cannot leave till the judgment day.

Yes, she hears again that cry!
 Hears lady Janet, May Jean;
She sees by the bedside the fardel lie,
With a gentle-faced grey ghost standing by;—
 Are they not really gone who die?
She shakes back her tresses, she lifts her hand,
For holy water she had at command,
To scald the wicked like hot sand.
 There's no lamp-light where spirits lie.

'Receive it back,' the grey ghost cried,
 'Sweet lady Janet, May Jean!

I too, long ago, before I died,
Threw the loud-tongued new life from my side ; '—
  Once the clock strikes, never more.
' Begone ! ' sore troubled, she tried to say,
' Sweet-tongued ghost-woman, hide it away,
Hide it for ever before it is day ! '
  Voices pass from shore to shore.

Again she 's alone, and within that bower,
  The lady Janet, May Jean,
Lays down her head for another hour,
Listens and looks through the walls of the tower ;—
  The bell-ringer mounts the spire-stair.
Why is her heart in her eye and ear,
Whence is the fever, and whence the fear,
When the bolt is drawn and no one near ?
Hears she or sees she anything ?
The moth at last hath burned its wing :
  Clang o' the matin is heard i' the air.

She hears still nearer that new-born cry,
  Hears lady Janet, May Jean ;
She sees close to her the fardel lie,
With Mary the Blessèd May standing by,
  In an arbour of white lilies great and high ;—
  The light should burn bright on the altar.
Then Mary the Blest bent down and undid
The swathes of linen that were its bed,
And took in her hand the small child's head.
  Now the quire-leader opens the psalter.

'Welcome!' said she, 'my son's young brother;
   Dear lady Janet, May Jean,
 Here is the God's-gift, His and no other,
To be thine for ever, thou May and yet mother!'
   The new day's dawning spreadeth wide.

 Is it but now that her eyes unclose,
 That she first sees the small face like a rose
 Upon her own white breast repose?
   Sunrise clouds have gold inside.

KRIEMHILD'S TRYSTE.

I

CHILDE ERIC from the Middle-sea
　　Rides on his homeward way,
To keep his tryste with fair Kriemhild,
　　His tryste of an early day.

Childe Eric rides by the swift running beck,
    Its sound fills all the air;
It is warm in the midsummer weather;
    It is noon, he will rest him there.

He throws the rein of his good roan steed
    On the bough of a sycamore,
And, dropping from brae to bank, he gains
    The linn-pool's pebbly shore.

He had travelled far from morn till noon,
    The fresh stream danced and sang,
So to cast his surcoat and hose of mail
    He did not question lang.

Then caroll'd he loud as the water,
    So bright, so fresh, so full;
His shapely waist and fair broad chest
    Flashed in the quivering pool.

But scarcely had he stept three steps,
    He heard a low shrill call,
And when he stept again there came
    A laugh from the waterfall.

And he saw within the rainbow mist,
    Within the shimmering vail,
A naked woman watching him,
    Breathless and rosy-pale.

Two heavy sheaves of golden hair
    About her round loins met,
Yet, for all the waters falling,
    These thick locks were not wet.

Her great kind eyes, her wild sweet eyes,
    They smiled and loved him so,
He shrank back in bewilderment,
    Yet had no wish to go.

But he felt sure that bonnie brown quean
    Was none of Eve's true kin :
Naked and unabashed, straight and frank,
    Harboured within the linn.

Silenced, with wandering wits he stood,
    His fair limbs but half hid,
Then stretched his hand from rock to rock,
    And backward sloped and slid.

But suddenly to the waist he sank,
    And forward sprang the maid,
Round either side his tingling waist
    Her arms a girdle made.

Then breast to breast in the cool water
    Was warmly, blindly pressed,
And heart to heart, as love is born,—
    Her great clear eyes confessed

An innocence and a childish joy,
    And hope's most flattering song,
That he, as was his wont with maids,
    Was reassured and strong.

At once he kissed her eager mouth—
    It was a quivering, wildering kiss—
Tighter she strained him in her arms,
    And fixed devouring lips on his.

And owned that she had waited long
    For him, Childe Eric, him alone;
But he must swear her troth, and be,
    As Holy Writ says, bone of bone.

As she had heard the priest declare,
    When she hid by the chapel door,
And he told them all of Adam and Eve—
    The old priest of Felsenore.

'I'll bring you luck, you'll bring me grace,
    And we'll be marrows, you and me;
A wife and a mother, my long hair coiffed,
    Clad in long-lawn and cramoisie.'

Yes, yes, his troth—as he had done
    In eastern lands before,
To dark eyes and brown jewelled ears—
    He pledged it o'er and o'er.

'Oh, then baptise me, Childe Delight!
    Madonna Mary, christen me!'—
The water now wet her sheaves of hair,
    And he laughed at her pietiè.

For he trusted in magic, and had come
    Through Rome, that evil vale,
Where with the false pope Archimed
    He had quaffed from the Holy Graal.

He laughed—but is not that his hound's
    Long howl above the brae?
And is not that his good roan steed—
    What maketh it stamp and neigh?

Oh, she was lissom and fond and strong,
    Guileless and wild and free;
Nor had she even a thought uncouth
    Lying under the rowan tree.

He was Eric the tall, from Mickle-garth,
    Her husband and paramour;
And she was a wife now, body and soul,
    So thoughtful and demure.

The manyfold kisses, and new sweet speech,
    That four lips feel like fire;
The thirsting heart and the hungry eyes,
    Why must they ever tire?

But all things else, all fair things else,
    The sun and his fruits also,
The birds and leaves, the flowers and sheaves,
    They change, and they may go.

Into that warm nest, filled with song
    By the lark and the murmuring linn,
Nought living came; but the pensive eye
    Of a white doe once looked in.

They slept, I think, till all at once
    He rose with a start and stare,
Like a man who knew not where he was,
    Nor how he had come there,
And climbed the bank and found his steed
    Had cropped all round it bare.

Sadly it turned its proud arched neck,
    And tried to lick his hand,
So he mounted in haste, and gallop'd away
    To the lady Kriemhild's land.

But he had sworn he would return,
    Return to the May, had he,
With a ring, and a necklace, and girdle-gold,
    And long-lawn and cramoisie.

II

Beyond the sound of the widening beck
    He rode to the river strand,
And at her bower-door on the island
    He saw the good Kriemhild stand.

Behind her too, on either side,
    Her bower-maids, a sister pair,
Clad both the same in sea-green serge,
    Trimmed with the minnevair.

But her long waist was in white say,
    Looped up with knops of gold;
For she was the heiress of the land,
    And towns with garth and wold.

Along yon further shore you see
    Her castle walls and tower;
But she had planned the tryste to be
    Within her island-bower.

So these green-kirtled serving-maids,
    They ferried him o'er the tide;—
As he leaned and looked in the tangled deep,
    What was it he descried?

What was it? for he backward shrank,
   And made the light bark sway,
Till it grated against the landing steps,—
   He seemed to have lost his way.

The lady then came stepping down
   Towards him in surprise;
Sudden he seized her two white hands,
   And bowed to hide his eyes.

With that the distant warder blew
   A note from the highest tower;
Startled, he kissed her two white hands,
   And they passed within the bower.

'I wonder much,' quoth fair Joanne
   To her sister Claribee,
'What made him wince when that great fish
   Swam up so bonnily?'

Each side the door then sat they down,
   With lutes of cedar wood;
Joan sang this song, and Claribee,
   She made the refrain good.

Quoth the wanderer, I have journeyed far,
Oh, give me wine and bread!
     Is the popinjay merry?

I have broken the bread and drank the wine,
I prithee now make my bed ;
> *The heart is as cold as stone.*

For, alas! I am wounded deep and sore,
And you must salve my wound :
> *Is the popinjay merry ?*

With her balsam sweet that lady-leech
She made him whole and sound.
> *The heart is as cold as stone.*

Anon, when again he was whole and well,
He said she must marry him ;
> *Is the popinjay merry ?*

And so it fell out that she called the priest,
All in the twilight dim.
> *The heart is as cold as stone.*

But when the wedding-ring touched her hand,
I must leave you, love, quoth he ;
> *Is the popinjay merry ?*

For I have a wife in a far-off town,
Across the weary sea.
> *The heart is as cold as stone.*

But she would not now by wind or wave
That he should go away ;
> *Is the popinjay merry ?*

So she made Sir Merlin weave a spell,
He could not choose but stay.
> *The heart is as cold as stone.*

Nor could he remember ever more,
Though he strove with might and main;
   Is the popinjay merry?
The wife he had left in the far-off land
He never would see again.
   The heart is as cold as stone.

Scarce ended they, a quivering flame
 Winnowed the sultry air,
And a surf running up as from sea-wind
 Lapped the green margin there.

The damsels laughed at the silvery foam
 That ran back again as fast;
Then tightened the cords of their gitterns,
 And sang against the blast:
But as they sang a darkness fell,
 And hail-stones rattled past.

HÆC.

Rest ye now from all your pain,
My heart's delight, my found-again.

ILLE.

Found again, but full of pyne
Thou art also, mistress mine.

HÆC.

Yea, but now we'll make amend;
The years of tears have reached their end.

ILLE.

Tears and years—oh, many a one
Since my wand'rings were begun!

HÆC.

Wanderings here and there away,
Never done at close of day.

ILLE.

Never done, but hankering still
For the old days of wild freewill.

HÆC.

Childish days when, ages gone,
We foster-children lived alone.

ILLE.

Lived and loved, for then we knew
Where the sweetest apple grew.

HÆC.

But once, alas! you plucked it down,
And wrapt it in my guiltless gown.

ILLE.

Plucked and shared it, rind and core;
Yet the sun set as before.

HÆC.

The sun set, but it rose no more ;
It went down, and life shut the door.

ILLE.

Shut, but we shall entrance gain ;—
Behold ! the sun wakes up again.

HÆC.

Another sweet apple upon the tree—
Lovers in dead years, can they see ?

ILLE.

See and pluck, rind, core, and pips,
Part and share with hungry lips.

HÆC.

Part and share, but alas ! it drips—
Drips with blood,—My heart's delight !
Our hearts are torn in mirk midnight.

III

Therewith a cry shot over them,
   As it came from out the sea—
The cry of a woman in sharp despite,
   Crying, 'Aï, woe is me !'

The hail it flashed on bench and board,
    By a loud wind borne along;
The singers fled within the bower,
    And thrust the bolt so strong.

And there the lady Kriemhild sat,
    Childe Eric by her side,—
Together sat they hand in hand,
    But their eyes were turned aside.

And the damsels knew as she sat so still,
    With never a welcome word,
Their ditty had shorn between them
    As it had been a sword.

They too were foster-children once,
    Their love too had been strong,—
Can what hath passed return again
    Like the burden of a song?

For Love descends with a great surprise,
    An angel on our cold floor;
And he never should leave us, never again,
    For we're colder than before.

Was this the boy she played with once
    Come from the great war's game,
More learned too than a priest, 'twas said,—
    While she remained the same?

It seemed as she sat, long miles away
    Some wedding-bells rang out;
But whether for her or for some other bride,
    She mazed herself in doubt.

Whose were they if they were not hers?
    Some dream she would recall;
But the gathering thunder swept them out,
    And shook the wainscot wall.

Then again that wild lamenting cry,
    'Aï, oh, woe is me!'
Severed the air like a fiery lance;—
    Nor could she choose but see
It went right through him like his doom,—
    'Aï, oh, woe is me!'

And with it rolled a surge of waves
    All round the bower outside;
A knocking smote the bolted door,
    The voice behind it cried:—

'Come back to me, Eric! I am now
    A woman with love in store;—
Why went you while I slept?—my hair
    Is not now as heretofore.

'It clings so heavy and cold and wet,
    Oh, hasten, and bring with thee
The ring and the necklace and girdle-gold,
    The long-lawn and cramoisie!

'My guardian and my husband sworn,
    Return again to me,
And these sea-waters will go back,
    Back safe into the sea.

'The rain it runs down breast and thigh,—
    For thee I am so brave:
I would not that mine ancient kin
    Shall make the floods thy grave!'

The gentle Kriemhild and her maids
    Together stood quite still,
Stood altogether listening
    To the voice so wild and shrill.

'Childe Eric, oh my long-betrothed,
    Who is this calling so?'
'Alas! I know not nor can tell,
    And you must never know.'

'My sweet bower-maidens, tell me true,
    Who is it calleth him?'
'I see,' quoth Joan, 'by the window-pane
    A brown sea-serpent swim——'

'But we must mount the topmost steps,
    The flood-waves rise so high,'—
'I cannot move,' Childe Eric cries;
    'I must remain to die.'

With that she fell upon his neck,
    She would not leave him there;
But her damsels raised her in their arms,
    And clomb the higher stair.

And as they climbed they heard below
    The door wide open fly;
Then all at once the darkness broke
    Across the rending sky,

And struggling strongly out, they saw,
    Amidst the coiling spray,
A long-haired woman's shining arms,
    Wherein Childe Eric lay!

And faintly came again that cry,
    'Aï, oh, woe is me!
Where is the ring and the girdle-gold,
    The long-lawn and cramoisie?'

WOODSTOCK MAZE.

'O NEVER shall anyone find you then!'
　Said he, merrily pinching her cheek;
'But why?' she asked,—he only laughed,—
　'Why shall it be thus, now speak!'

'Because so like a bird art thou,
   Thou must live within green trees,
With nightingales and thrushes and wrens,
   And the humming of wild bees.'
      Oh, the shower and the sunshine every day
      Pass and pass, be ye sad, be ye gay.

'Nay, nay, you jest, no wren am I,
   Nor thrush nor nightingale,
And rather would keep this arras and wall
   'Tween me and the wind's assail.
I like to hear little Minnie's gay laugh,
   And the whistle of Japes the page,
Or to watch old Madge when her spindle twirls,
   And she tends it like a sage.'
      Oh, the leaves, brown, yellow, and red, still fall,
      Fall and fall over churchyard or hall.

'Yea, yea, but thou art the world's best Rose,
   And about thee flowers I'll twine,
And wall thee round with holly and beech,
   Sweet-briar and jessamine.'
'Nay, nay, sweet master, I'm no Rose,
   But a woman indeed, indeed,
And love many things both great and small,
   And of many things more take heed.'
      Oh, the shower and the sunshine every day
      Pass and pass, be ye sad, be ye gay.

'Aye, sweetheart, sure thou sayest sooth,
   I think thou art even so!
But yet needs must I dibble the hedge,
   Close serried as hedge can grow.
Then Minnie and Japes and Madge shall be
   Thy merry-mates all day long,
And thou shalt hear my bugle-call
   For matin or even-song.'
     Oh, the leaves, brown, yellow, and red, still fall,
     Fall and fall over churchyard or hall.

Look yonder now, my blue-eyed bird,
   See'st thou aught by yon far stream?
There shalt thou find a more curious nest
   Than ever thou sawest in dream.'
She followed his finger, she looked in vain,
   She saw neither cottage nor hall,
But at his beck came a litter on wheels,
   Screened by a red silk caul;
He lifted her in by her lily-white hand,
   So left they the blythe sunny wall.
     Oh, the shower and the sunshine every day
     Pass and pass, be ye sad, be ye gay.

The gorse and ling are netted and strong,
   The conies leap everywhere,
The wild briar-roses by runnels grow thick;
   Seems never a pathway there.

Then come the dwarf oaks knotted and wrung
    Breeding apples and mistletoe,
And now tall elms from the wet mossed ground
    Straight up to the white clouds go.
        Oh, the leaves, brown, yellow, and red, still fall,
        Fall and fall over churchyard or hall.

'O weary hedge, O thorny hedge!'
    Quoth she in her lonesome bower,
'Round and round it is all the same;
    Days, weeks, have all one hour;
I hear the cushat far overhead,
    From the dark heart of that plane;
Sudden rushes of wings I hear,
    And silence as sudden again.
        Oh, the shower and the sunshine every day
        Pass and pass, be ye sad, be ye gay.

'Maiden Minnie she mopes by the fire,
    Even now in the warmth of June;
I like not Madge to look in my face,
    Japes now hath never a tune.
But, oh, he is so kingly strong,
    And, oh, he is kind and true;
Shall not my babe, if God cares for me,
    Be his pride and his joy too?
        Oh, the leaves, brown, yellow, and red, still fall,
        Fall and fall over churchyard or hall.

I lean my faint heart against this tree
   Whereon he hath carved my name,
I hold me up by this fair bent bough,
   For he held once by the same;
But everything here is dank and cold,
   The daisies have sickly eyes,
The clouds like ghosts down into my prison
   Look from the barred-out skies.
     Oh, the shower and the sunshine every day
     Pass and pass, be ye sad, be ye gay.

' I tune my lute and I straight forget
   What I minded to play, woe's me!
Till it feebly moans to the sharp short gusts
   Aye rushing from tree to tree.
Often that single redbreast comes
   To the sill where my Jesu stands;
I speak to him as to a child; he flies,
   Afraid of these poor thin hands!
     Oh, the leaves, brown, yellow, and red, still fall,
     Fall and fall over churchyard or hall.

' 'The golden evening burns right through
   My dark chamber windows twain:
I listen, all round me is only a grave,
   Yet listen I ever again.
Will he come? I pluck the flower-leaves off,
   And at each, cry, yes, no, yes!

I blow the down from the dry hawkweed,
   Once, twice, ah! it flyeth amiss!
     Oh, the shower and the sunshine every day
     Pass and pass, be ye sad, be ye gay.

' Hark! he comes! yet his footstep sounds
   As it sounded never before!
Perhaps he thinks to steal on me,
   But I'll hide behind the door.'
She ran, she stopped, stood still as stone—
   It was Queen Eleänore;
And at once she felt that it was death
   The hungering she-wolf bore!
     Oh, the leaves, brown, yellow, and red, still fall,
     Fall and fall over churchyard or hall.

THE WITCH'S BALLAD.

O, I HAE come from far away,
    From a warm land far away,
A southern land across the sea,
With sailor-lads about the mast,
Merry and canny, and kind to me.

And I hae been to yon town,
    To try my luck in yon town;
Nort, and Mysie, Elspie too.
Right braw we were to pass the gate,
Wi' gowden clasps on girdles blue.

Mysie smiled wi' miminy mouth,
    Innocent mouth, miminy mouth;
Elspie wore her scarlet gown,
Nort's grey eyes were unco' gleg,
My Castile comb was like a crown.

We walked abreast all up the street,
    Into the market up the street;
Our hair with marygolds was wound,
Our bodices with love-knots laced,
Our merchandise with tansy bound.

Nort had chickens, I had cocks,
    Gamesome cocks, loud-crowing cocks ;
Mysie ducks, and Elspie drakes,—
For a wee groat or a pound :
We lost nae time wi' gives and takes.

Lost nae time, for well we knew,
    In our sleeves full well we knew,
When the gloaming came that night,
Duck nor drake nor hen nor cock
Would be found by candle-light.

And when our chaffering all was done,
    All was paid for, sold and done,
We drew a glove on ilka hand,
We sweetly curtsied each to each,
And deftly danced a saraband.

The market lasses looked and laughed,
    Left their gear and looked and laughed ;
They made as they would join the game,
But soon their mithers, wild and wud,
With whack and screech they stopped the same.

Sae loud the tongues o' randies grew,
    The flitin' and the skirlin' grew,
At all the windows in the place,
Wi' spoons or knives, wi' needle or awl,
Was thrust out every hand and face.

And down each stair they thronged anon,
　　Gentle, semple, thronged anon;
Souter and tailor, frowsy Nan,
The ancient widow young again,
Simpering behind her fan.

Without a choice, against their will,
　　Doited, dazed, against their will,
The market lassie and her mither,
The farmer and his husbandman,
Hand in hand dance a' thegether.

Slow at first, but faster soon,
　　Still increasing wild and fast,
Hoods and mantles, hats and hose,
Blindly doffed and cast away,
Left them naked, heads and toes.

They would have torn us limb from limb,
　　Dainty limb from dainty limb;
But never one of them could win
Across the line that I had drawn
With bleeding thumb a-widdershin.

But there was Jeff the provost's son,
　　Jeff the provost's only son;
There was Father Auld himsel',
The Lombard frae the hostelry,
And the lawyer Peter Fell.

All goodly men we singled out,
    Waled them well, and singled out,
And drew them by the left hand in;
Mysie the priest, and Elspie won
The Lombard, Nort the lawyer carle,
I mysel' the provost's son.

Then, with cantrip kisses seven,
    Three times round with kisses seven,
Warped and woven there spun we,
Arms and legs and flaming hair,
Like a whirlwind on the sea.

Like the wind that sucks the sea,
    Over and in and on the sea,
Good sooth it was a mad delight;
And every man of all the four
Shut his eyes and laughed outright.

Laughed as long as they had breath,
    Laughed while they had sense or breath;
And close about us coiled a mist
Of gnats and midges, wasps and flies,
Like the whirlwind shaft it rist.

Drawn up I was right off my feet,
    Into the mist and off my feet;
And, dancing on each chimney-top,
I saw a thousand darling imps
Keeping time with skip and hop.

And on the provost's brave ridge-tile,
    On the provost's grand ridge-tile,
The Blackamoor first to master me
I saw,—I saw that winsome smile,
The mouth that did my heart beguile,
And spoke the great Word over me,
In the land beyond the sea.

I called his name, I called aloud,
    Alas! I called on him aloud;
And then he filled his hand with stour,
And threw it towards me in the air;
My mouse flew out, I lost my pow'r!

My lusty strength, my power, were gone;
    Power was gone, and all was gone.
He will not let me love him more!
Of bell and whip and horse's tail
He cares not if I find a store.

But I am proud if he is fierce!
    I am as proud as he is fierce;
I'll turn about and backward go,
If I meet again that Blackamoor,
And he'll help us then, for he shall know
I seek another paramour.

And we'll gang once more to yon town,
    Wi' better luck to yon town;
We'll walk in silk and cramoisie,
And I shall wed the provost's son;
My-lady of the town I'll be!

For I was born a crowned king's child,
    Born and nursed a king's child,
King o' a land ayont the sea,
Where the Blackamoor kissed me first,
And taught me art and glamourie.

Each one in her wame shall hide
    Her hairy mouse, her wary mouse,
Fed on madwort and agramie,—
Wear amber beads between her breasts,
And blind-worm's skin about her knee.

The Lombard shall be Elspie's man,
    Elspie's gowden husband-man;
Nort shall take the lawyer's hand;
The priest shall swear another vow:
We'll dance again the saraband!

SAINT MARGARET.

The wan lights freeze on the dark cold floor,
Witch lights and green the high windows adorn ;
The cresset is gone out the altar before,
She knows her long hour of life's nigh worn,
And she kneels here waiting to be re-born,
        On the stones of the chancel.

' That door darkly golden, that noiseless door,
Through which I can see sometimes,' said she,
' Will it ever be opened to close no more ;
Will those wet clouds cease pressing on me ;
Shall I cease to hear the sound of the sea ?'
        Her handmaids miss her and rise.

' I've served in life's prison-house long,' she said,
' Where silver and gold are heavy and bright,
Where children wail and where maidens wed,
Where the day is wearier than the night,
And each would be master if he might.'
        Margaret ! they seek thee.

The night waxed darker than before;
Scarce could the windows be traced at all,
Only the sharp rain was heard rushing o'er;
A sick sleeper moaned through the cloister wall,
And a horse neighed shrill from a distant stall,
         And the sea sounded on.

'Are all the dear holy ones shut within,
That none descend in my strait?' said she;
'Their songs are afar off, far off and thin,
The terrible sounds of the prison-house flee
About me, and the sound of the sea.'
         Lights gleam from room to room.

Slowly a moonshine breaks over the glass,
The black and green witchcraft is there no more;
It spreads and it brightens, and out of it pass
Four angels with glorified hair,—all four
With lutes; and our Lord is in heaven's door.
         Margaret! they hail thee.

Her eyes are a-wide to the hallowèd light,
Her head is cast backward, her bosom is clad
With the flickering moonlight pale purple and white;
Away to the angels her spirit hath fled,
While her body still kneels,—but is it not dead?
         She is safe, she is well!

THE RENDEZVOUS.

' Lay my head upon thy neck,
   My sister, ever so dear to me;
Thy cool cheek on my burning brow,
   And if I weep, you may not see.
      The wind it lies i' the sedges.

' In this low shieling down so far,
   Below the bower where we were born,
He knows I'll wait to hear again
   The sound o' his blythe bugle-horn.
      The wind it sighs i' the sedges.

' I hold him blameless now as then,
   For love must bide with confidence,
And truth with trust I surely think,
   Withouten question or defence.
      The wind it sings i' the sedges.

' Here, sheltered in the thick green shaw,
   The day is long, the night is drear;
But days and nights wear on until
   The joy of his return is near.
      The wind it clings to the sedges.

THE RENDEZVOUS.

'As I stood on the wrinkled shore
   The waves they sang of him to me,
Here-away, there-away, wandering
   On the far side of the sea.
      Butterflies light on the sedges.

'They said his dark days all were done,
   And that his ship was in full sail,
With men on the deck and wealth below,
   And braws for me, the pick and wale.
      The lily is bright in the sedges.

'So here I've come to this dear place,
   And yestere'en the high window,
Where we in one bed children slept,
   I saw it shining in the glow.
      The small fish darts i' the sedges.

'It seemed in fancy I discerned
   The place where once our two heads lay,
And I thought how oft you combed my hair,
   And dressed me many a day.
      The bittern starts i' the sedges.

'For thou wert ever a mother to me;
   I, weak and wayward, scarce can tell
How good thou wert,—and yet I went
   That dreadful night without farewell.
      The badger rattles the sedges.

' But I so feared our father, Maud ;
  Love-wildered, I had lost my head :
I feared still more that false Delue
  My father meant that I should wed.'
    The bind-weed wattles the sedges.

' Ah, well-a-day ! my sister May,
  I shrink from him as then you did ;
For now he is to husband me,
  If I conform, as I am bid.'
    The adder it hides i' the sedges.

' But that must never, never be ;
  Wise sister Maud, it shall not be :
For, hark ! my true love's bugle-note—
  I know it brings good cheer to me !'
    Sunlight glides through the sedges.

' Nay, 'tis but father's hunting-horn,
  With horses, dogs, and false Delue !'
' They also ! but by yon cross road
  There comes my love, and his men too !
    The wind again breaks i' the sedges.

' And now I know the hour shall strike,
  Cast out my child and I shall be ;
Or false Delue's last game is played ;—
  We'll part no more, my love and me !
    The spring it awakes i' the sedges.

'Now they parley, man to man,—
  Short speech, alas! for they must fight:
My Lionel and Delue,—at once
  They draw their swords, so long and brigh
    The fisherman watches the sedges.

'My father and that stranger lord
  Draw back the men each side the way,
Some here, some there, they stand in line,
  Stand to look, as it were play!
    The hurricane catches the sedges.

'My sister Maud, now hold me up;
  I must stand here, I must look on,—
Holy Mary, soothe my child
  Until this mortal strife be done!
    The storm wind weighs on the sedges.

'I must look on,—fear not for me;
  Full well I know his arm is strong:
I must look on,—full well I know
  The struggle will not hold them long.
    The wild wind lays down the sedges.

'My child, my child! so loud it cries,
  I pressed it all too close to me;
He hears it, and he turns this way,
  His hand drops down beside his knee.
    The lightning shatters the sedges.

'Delue is closing on him now;—
  My true, true love, it never can be!
Take me, sister, in your arms;
  I cannot hear, I cannot see.'
    The flood-tide scatters the sedges.

'Lie down, lie down! and let me watch:
  Delue goes back with deadly wound;
He tries in vain to lift his arm,—
  He falls—falls flat upon the ground.
    The rain it spurns the sedges.

'Hear you, sister, what I say?
  Shouts and steps approach the door:
'Tis Lionel himself who lifts you,
  Gently lifts you from the floor!'
    Sunshine returns to the sedges.

'I GO TO BE CURED AT AVILION.'

(To a Picture painted 1847.)

SILENTLY, swiftly the funeral barge
Homeward bears the brave and good,
His wide pall sweeping the murmuring marge,
 Flowing to the end of the world.
Kings' daughters watching round his head,
His brazen breastplate wet with blood
And tears by these kings' daughters shed,
 Watching to the end of the world.

A cresset of spices and sandal-wood
Fills the wake with an odour rare ;
Two swans lead dimly athwart the flood,
 Lead on to the end of the world.
From the distant wold what brings the blast?
The trump's recall, the watch-fire's glare,—
Oh ! let these fade into the past,
 As he fares to the end of the world.

From the misty woods a holier sound—
For the monks are singing their evensong—
Swoons faintly o'er the harvest-ground,
   As they pass to the end of the world.
From the minster where the steep roofs are,
The passing bell, that voice supreme,
Sends a farewell faintly far,
   As they fade to the end of the world.

It is gone, it is closed, the last red gleam,
Darkness shuts the fiery day ;
Over the windless, boatless stream
The odours and embers have died away :
   They are gone to the end of the world.

ANTHONY.

A.D. 1000.

'And the Lord said unto Satan, Behold, he is in thy hand.'
JOB ii. 6.

 'FATHER, my quiet life hath lain
 In the hollows where the dews and rain
 From one day into another remain,
  Cold and green.   One sin alone
 Up through my peace like a thorn hath grown :

I have tried to be humble in vain; I've thought
More of my gifts than a poor child ought;
I have believed to me was given
The powers of the Saints—of miracles even;
And I fear me Jesu hath sent his leven
To burn away the crown of pride
That, try as I might, I never could hide.
And to bear the great God's chastening,
With the bodily sense, is a fearful thing!

' Father dear, last night I woke
As a hand was gently laid on me,
And a soft voice close beside me spoke :
" Good brother, brother Anthony,
A king is dying here close by,
And wants thy ghostly aid." I rose
Upon mine elbow 'mazedly ;
This beggar-voice, whose could it be?
Who could have come where no path goes,
Among the shingle and birks that close
My cell about? A faint light made
By the moon there was, and across it a shade
Moved ; from behind me a face right fair
Suddenly stooped, half hid by its hair,
Yet round the white brow might be seen
A fretted gold thread. "Come, brother," quoth he,
" Or death before us may have been ".——
" Nay, I ween it must not be :

To deal out God's body to the dying,
To sain the soul through the dark night flying,
I'm powerless.   I'm no priest : go round
To the Clerk of Isenford."   "That ground
I travelled now ; but it is said
That yesternight the clerk is dead."
"Then mount ye the hill to the cenoby."
" Time is too short," he made reply ;
And got the better of me then,
I thought myself singled out among men,
Appointed by the Saints to do
This holy thing : I rise and go ;
The pax ye left last yule with me
I put in my bosom hastily ;
I follow him along by the river.   Anon
He opened a door in a garden wall,
And muttered some words I can't recall,
Then stept we down long steps of stone,
Still down and evermore downwards—dark
It was, and yet I heard, by chance,
As we spoke together, the early lark ;
Anon it seemed as if I must dance,
Not walk, so giddy and light was I ;
And then there seemed to be houses round,
Unsteadily resting on the ground,
As if they but seemed, and might change or fly ;
With pictures were they painted o'er,
And settles stood by every door.

Past these we went, I following him,
The heavy heat making my head to swim
As if I were drunken. Then came a sound,
The regular chaunt of a litany—
Doubtless to Hecat or Venus—and they
Who chanted it were seen nowhere,
Neither on ground nor in the air:
Nor was there green field or blue sky,
Or tree or stream, but all was brown,
And flames like lamps leapt up and down:
Nor saw I aught living in doublet or gown,
Till we came to the market-place, where stood,
Instead of a cross, an image of wood,
A huge-faced image, with ass's ears,
And horns and a tongue and eyes full of leers,
Bodyless, only a block, whence grew
Lopped arms and shameless parts—before
The image flickered a flame dark blue,
And round it, hand in hand, a score
Of dark brown men and women ran,
Naked as devils: I tried to ban;
I had no book or cross, but the pax,
With the blessed body sealed in silver and wax!
The pax was gone, and that was how
They gained such power upon me now.
My winsome guide laid hold on me,
Capering as if his bare feet were on thorns;
But the beauty, I trow, was quite gone now—

I saw he too had horns !
Oh, had I at the first but seen
The fire in his eyen—oh, well had it been !
Alas ! how they did pierce and play
About me and into me, into my heart !
And the place wherever he made them dart
Was lit up by a quivering gleam,
Like that from sunlit glass or stream.
I turned and ran ; but round and round
Still danced the fiends till I fell in a swound,
And I woke anon where about me, I trow,
Was kingly ornament enow :
On a couch of gold, on a tiger's hide,
I lay, and a creature meek and mild,
Wimpled like a sister of Transatide,
Smoothed my hair down like a child,
And laid my face against her side.
Oh, but it was strange and new,
The unrest that within me grew :
I believed her a sister—some glamour,
Some smoke of the pit, some nameless power,
Was there ; but I prevailed at last !
Her arms about my head she cast ;
" I am a princess," the serpent said,
Ere you arrived was my father dead ;
And you must now rule here, for I
Can give you knowledge and sovereignty,
With a crown to cover your tonsured head."

Woe's me ! I listened, sorry and sad
That she was a devil or I was mad :
I lay still and listened, and then she drew
From a small red distaff that stood by itself,
And moved to her hand like a living elf,
A fine green thread she cunningly threw
Around me and round. Then a can of green flame
Or of wine—I knew not whence it came—
She called it wine—to my mouth she pressed,
And whispered so softly, " Drink now, and rest."
I was wearing to sleep, and my lips were dry ;
A want, not of will, but of energy,
Was saving me, till at last she sung—
Thank thee, O thou foolish red tongue !

   Is there a better place over the sky?
   Is there a fairer race living on high?
   Is there a hell, can any man tell?
   For he knoweth nought when the shroud is wrought;
   But I've heard it said by the midday breeze,
   In the churchyard trees, and by the grey seas,
   Upon midsummer night, when the moon is in flight,
   That Paradise is but a shade
   Made by the evening clouds in the air,
   A delusion and a snare.
   So brother dear, oh, harbour here,
   And live with me ; for a mortal year
   Will be nothing to thee, if thou wilt not tine
   The offer of my bright green wine.

I tried right sore, but no word could say,
While she touched me, that accursed May,
With her thread and her wine,—I feared them now,
And she knew the fear upon my brow;
I saw her trembling through her hair,
And then at once I was aware
That she was changed or gone; for there,
Instead of her, another stood,
Also clad in a wimple and hood;
My book and my beads, with the little black rood,
She held towards me, and she sung
With a sharp clear voice, and a bright red tongue:
    Nay, look not so, for it grieves us mo'
    Than I can tell, and of heaven and hell,
    What they are made of, and where they lie,
    And how to find them by-and-by,
    Thou shalt teach, and we shall hear—
I broke upon her silly song
By grasping at the hallowed gear;—
Ah, when I found it in my grasp,
The rood was changed into an asp.
But the thread was broken, and I was strong,
For I struggled up and out of her reach;
I found my voice,—that vile asp tried
To get into my mouth,—but three times I cried
Upon the name of Christ—the wall
About me splits, and the devils fall
And break like images of board,—
Such is the power of the name of the Lord!

'Long I threaded the streets about,
That I might find some pathway out;
Nor could I tell the west from east:
So I was lost.   By many a door
Fallen, and many a settle before,
The naked creatures broken lay,
Like sculptor's fragments cast away.
And yet their eyes could follow me,
Although they could not move or turn;
I stumbled over them; I could spurn
Their breasts and limbs,—but those wide-open eyes!
Ah, me! at last I saw on high
This hill against the morning sky;—
Was it not hard from thence to see
This chapel at hand, and between it and me—
Enchantment—like a wall of glass,
It seemed I never, never could pass?
Then I remembered the spell whereby
The possessed wherever they list can fly;
That spell brother Lupus, cursed be he!
Brought from the pagans of Sicily:
And I was lifted from the ground,
Bats and ribbed things clipping me round,
And thrown down; then, oh! such a race
I ran,—for everything gave me chase,
Wolves, moles, birds, stones, hosts of flies;
And the faces of women and men I know
Died many and many a year ago,

Kept up with me, their white, light eyes
Close to my face; all vampires, so
They bit my neck, they sucked my blood,
They caught my ankles, they twisted my hood,
And at last—at last they stole
My senses; without sense I ran,
Like a jointed frame without a soul;
Yet I knew the joints, alas! began
To double and crack;—but oh! God's bliss!
About my feet a stream doth hiss,
The cold, running stream, and I am free,
With daylight, father, and with thee!'

II

When the stricken child had thus confessed,
Humbly he crossed his hands on his breast,
Waiting. The abbot raised his eyen,
That closèd this half-hour had been,
And answered: 'Thy name, Anthony,
Was once borne by a Saint; if so
It be with thee as with him, and mo',
Whom Jesu put in Satan's power
To bait them for a day and hour,
It doth behove thee back to go
Into thy hermitage again;
And if from grace thou art astray,
Anthony, gird thyself amain

With prayer and fast; this penance do,
And when thou vanquishest the foe,
Thou shalt rule, and I obey!'

He turned about, but the kneeling man
Caught the skirt of his camlet and began
To wail like the stork in the fowler's hand:
'Father! aught but this demand
Let me but live in the cenoby,
And penance day and night I'll dree;
Send me not to live alone——'
'The will of God, my will be done!'
Querulously the old man cried,
And thrust the penitent aside.

III

The sound of their parting steps is gone,
His heart sinks like his knees on the stone,
The asperging drops still shine on his head,
The smoke of the censer scarce is shed;
For they brought him hither with chant and bell,
Relics and incense-pot as well.
His long thin hands together are prest,
Finger to finger before his breast
  Through their closed lids you may see
  His eyeballs moving restlessly,

As if he listened with shut eyes,
For thus the senses sympathise!
And now he sings, but far to find
Is every rhyme he would unwind:

    Thou wood of the cross of the agony,
      Ye nails that fixed Him to the tree,
Sponge that held the last bitter draught,
      Lift, support, and strengthen me!

    Drops of His sweating that eased His pain,
      Drops of blood, the parched world's rain,
Tears that brought us man's second spring,
      Cleanse, absolve, absolve, and sain!

    Mary's most holy eyes then lifted up,
      Angels most holy hands holding the cup,
And Spirit most holy that then came down,
      Make my soul with ye to sup!

He stops, forgetting the rest; the lamp
Through its misty nimbus crackles; a tramp
Is heard without, a laugh and a call;—
He answers not: against the wall
All round the bigging the knocking goes,
From west to east as a witch-dance flows:
Then up on the thatch it begins to scratch;
There's a long thin line seen crossing the shrine,
Mistier still in the thickening damp;

By its dainty thread right over his head,
A spider spins, for a moment it stops,
Then right upon his bald head drops.
Ah! he comes as he came before,—
Only since they sprinkled the latch,
And set that cross upon the door,
He must enter by the thatch!
Anthony fell like a murdered man,
And that long-legged imp-spiderling ran
Over his face: now raised on his hands
He stares about, the hour-glass stands
Right upon end with its drizzling sands,
And the friendly mort-head, round and round
Rolls about with a crazy sound,
A gasping creak, it tries to speak,
Eyeballs from its caves gleam out!
The horns—the horns begin to sprout!

Next morn betimes they came to see
How fared their young brother Anthony,
But he was gone, nor could they trace
His footsteps nor his resting-place.

IV

'Tis well to spend the wintry day
Of age from tumults quite away:
When love is past, and we leave off strife,
Having long borne our lots in life.

Answering the daily need,
With brand and buckler to conquer or bleed;
Or for the burgher's watch so drear,
Filling the wallet with good cheer,
Or in the booth or market-stand
Where moil befits both tongue and hand:
But work is heavy from morn to eve,
With sorrow still watching behind like a reeve,
And the only shelter sure and fair
Is the cloister and cowl to the man of care,
To the man upon whom the great black hand
Of chastening waxeth tight, whose head
Is bowed, so he no more can stand
In the guild-hall he aforetime led.
Nor less to him who wickedly
Seeketh temptations, the lusts of the eye
And the pride of life; for surely God
Lends the heart a worm, the back a rod,
To punish those forgetting Him;
And His punishments are grim!
Abasing the haughty in velvet and fur,
Who hold their foreheads against the thunder,
And laugh to see the patched poor wonder,
Who travel with riders before and behind,
Riding over the halt and blind,
Who empty the stoup with the wassailer,
Over the chamber of the dying,—
Who wear the night with dice and lying,

Lying and cursing over the dice,
And to the chirp of the violette,
With a headless amorette
Dance until the cock crows thrice.

There was a time when Saints were rife,
Whose cross was ever their staff of life;
From Camelot to Egypt's river,
Blessings fell from Gabriel's quiver;
Nor was it wonderful to see
The holy rood stoop down to greet
The worshipper whose heart was sweet,
Whose deeds and thoughts did well agree,—
Who never dropt his beads to scratch,
Though his cassock was as coarse as thatch:
This age was likened to the sun
Upholding life since time begun.

Then glorious still, though glorious less,
The second age of holiness,
Was likened to the harvest-moon,
Whose sweet white face doth wane so soon.

Then came the third last age of light;
Darker it was, yet grand and bright,
Like the company of stars by night.

  But sun, and moon, and stars are gone,
And we the watchers left alone

With no more cheer than candlewick
Through a horn lantern, yellow and thick.
So now in the race, for one who wins,
Six shall stumble with wounded shins;
For the rood is stiff whoever kneels,
And God never stops His chariot wheels,
Nor looks out of His narrow window,
Over the drifts and steeps of snow;
But Satan for a thousand years
Has gotten a lease of our hopes and fears—
To catch men's souls by their eyes and ears.
Let us everyone beware
Little faith or overcaring,
Pride of heart or overdaring,
Lest we come within his snare.

In after years on that spot grew
Cloisters of stone all fair and new:
And Camaldules at least five-score
Lived where these few had housed before;
Then in the guest-hall oft was told
This story of the times of old,
And of a beggar-man, who lay
With crutch and cup by night and day,
Begging and muttering before
Saint Peter's great west door.
This beggar, when aught was flung in his cup,
If 'twas not silver would grumble and grutch,

And strive to raise his body up,
To reach the almoner with his crutch!
Then as the midnight struck, they said,
He lay stretched out as if he were dead,
When a hornèd stranger, strong and grim,
Through the locked city-gate came toward him,
And took his daily spoils away.
Some thought him a Saint, and gave him food
Day by day, as Christians should;
But others averred that Satan had
Sworn him his slave and driven him mad,
And that his name was Anthony.
But whether he was the same who fled
From his cell that night can never be said.

LOVE'S CALENDAR.

THAT gusty spring, each afternoon
   By the ivied cot I passed,
And noted at that lattice soon
   Her fair face downward cast;
Still in the same place seated there,
So diligent, so very fair.

Oft-times I said I knew her not,
   Yet that way round would go,
Until, when evenings lengthened out,
   And bloomed the may-hedge row,
I met her by the wayside well,
Whose waters, maybe, broke the spell.

For, leaning on her pail she prayed
   I'd lift it to her head,
So did I; but I'm much afraid
   Some wasteful drops were shed,
And that we blushed, as face to face
Needs must we stand the shortest space.

Then when the sunset mellowed through
    The ears of rustling grain,
When lattices wide open flew,
    When ash-leaves fell like rain,
As well as I she knew the hour
At morn or eve I neared her bower.

And now that snow o'erlays the thatch,
    Each starlit eve within
The door she waits, I raise the latch,
    And kiss her lifted chin;
Nor do I think we've blushed again,
For Love hath made but one of twain.

A BRIDAL RACE.

Sir Hubert mounted his little brown barb,
    Her jennette of Spain his bride;
'My winsome Isabelle, my wife,'
    Quoth he, 'let's a wager ride!'

Quoth he, 'Sweet wife, let us ride a race,
    And this shall be the play,
Whoever wins first to yon haw-tree,
    Shall do even as they may.

'And whether we live in the country,
    Or in town as I would still,
Whoever wins first to yon haw-tree
    Shall have it as they will.'

'Done!' said she with a light high laugh,
    'I'm pleased with such as this;
Let us sign the 'pact!' She leant across,
    As if she meant to kiss.

He thought to catch her limber waist,
  And really a kiss repay,
But she gave her jennette the rein at once ;
  She was off, she was away.

The little brown barb he shied aside,
  On galloped she merrilie,
The race was short and she was the first,
  First by the red haw-tree.

' Now fie upon you, winsome wife ! '
  Cried he, ' you ride unfair,
For with that feint, that start too soon,
  You took me unaware.'

' What's fair,' quoth she with her light high laugh,
  ' I do not care three straws !
Oh, I shall rule, yes, I shall rule,
  But you, love, shall make the laws ! '

PARTING AND MEETING AGAIN.

Last time I parted from my dear
The linnet sang from the briar-bush,
  The throstle from the dell;
The stream too carolled full and clear,
It was the spring-time of the year,
And both the linnet and the thrush
  I love them well,
Since last I parted from my dear.

But when he came again to me
The barley rustled high and low,
  Linnet and thrush were still;
Yellowed the apple on the tree,
'Twas autumn merry as it could be,
What time the white ships come and go
  Under the hill;
They brought him back again to me,
Brought him safely o'er the sea.

LOVE.

I LEFT the city gates. Through paths of sward,
Where never cloud of dust had fallen, I reached
An opening in a wall of sapling boughs;
I entered, and within more still and cool
It was, and freshness through the air exhaled
From the green ground. Half dusk it was, for round
And round the branches wove a screen from heaven
Of darkest green and varied leaf, 'neath which
Flies thickly humming danced. Sometimes a bird
Flew straightway through, and as its wing might brush
The leaves about your head, it seemed to fear
That it had missed its way. Flowers too were there,
Sprinkled about amidst the grass which grows
Hair-like and thin beneath the shade; bluebells
Tinkling to the small breeze a bee might cause,
And violets, and poppies red and rough
In stem. I passed still deeper through the wood
By this cool path: a wood more kindly cool,
Or harmless of dank poisons or vile beasts
That creep, there cannot be, and yet so wild
And uncouth. Bushes of dusk fruit beside

The pathway from the ground piled up two walls
Of leaves and berries, from which flocked the birds
As I passed on, or lingered with dyed hands
Plucking them listless, and with profuse waste
Pressing their juice out. Other trees were there
Blossoming for a later month. And now,
As from the populous harvest field came sounds
Of hearty laughter, till by distance lost,
And then again heard, as the reapers turned,
A snatch of song, a very pleasant sound,
Beneath a clear sky and thick boughs, a sound
Right happy. So I also sang. The sun
Then found an opening through the stems, to fall
Upon my path ; and as I walked across
The flowers upon my right my shadow passed.

A butterfly with purple-velvet wings,
Invested with two lines of dusky gold
And spotted with red spots, upon these flowers
Was feeding, and anon as my shade fell
Upon it, it flew up and went before,
Lighting again until I passed : and so
Continued it. The space more closed and closed
Became, and all between the trees were warped,
Hop-twigs and bindweed running far. Beneath,
A slow stream likewise glent, and secretly
Fed spreading water-lilies, and long reeds
Heavy with seed, which might have made fair pipes,

Cut nicely by the joints, from whence a leaf
Depended. But I thought not of the task,
Watching my guide's dark wings, until the path
Seemed stayed by dense convolvulus and may,
(Largely o'ergrown without the pruner's hands)
And wild white rose. But the dark sphynx-fly lowered
Its flight till nigh the ground, and passed into
The mass of greenery by an interspace
Unseen before ; with both my hands I raised,
And parted with my head, full lazily,
The luscious screen at this same interspace.

Behold ! beneath a peristyle I stand
Of short columnar palms, before me steps
Of fine-shorn grass descend unto a space
Carpeted, curtained, looped with garlands too,
And set all round with woven seats of boughs
Cut roughly from the forest, over which
Uptangling richly to the highest trees,
And waving then even into the air,
Were rare and unknown flowers, and round a fount
(Of which a marble girl, with green feet through
The water and white head, seemed Nymph) bright
      heaps
Of lily blooms were strewn. But all these things
After the first delight were nought to me ;
I was aware of some one near, whose life
The whole seemed imitative of, whose smile

The light seemed intimating to the flowers,
Whose graciousness all round seemed fashioned by.
Quite passively I stretched upon the sward,
Mazed by this unknown beauty, and the swarms
Of moths like that which here had guided me,
And then the influence became more clear,
More fixed, and I beheld a Lady. Round
Her hand, which held some sweet, the insects thronged,
And lighted on her hair. I did not start
With rapture nor surprise, nor did I deem
Myself unworthy of this gardened love,
This goddess-girl, nor said she aught to me;
But by her eyes, which never looked on me,
I said she was the spirit of my life,
And tho' I had not seen her until now,
I still had known her.

      She bent down beside
The sward I pressed; she leant on the rude seat
Over me; but I knew not from that hour,
Whether it was myself I gazed upon,
Or whether I beheld with love intense
And sympathy some higher beings, both
Worthy of each. And she began to sing;
A language which was song was hers,—she sang;
A fragile lute upon her knees she placed,
And, balanced from her neck by cord of silk,
Her fingers gave it speech, yet touched it not,

But her hands hovered o'er it like two birds
With wings still fluttering to descend,—she played.
Soft as the fine tints of a rainbow bound
About a shower that fell not: first her voice
Came on my sense, but scarce articulate;
Then, waxing louder, it ascended heaven
With all its colours brightening.   My heart
Is stilled to sleep as a maid stills a child
That murmurs not, but looks still upward on
The watching smile, till its eyes close at last
Unconsciously.   But suddenly the notes
Began to whirl together as a flight
Of swallows, and then louder still became,
Happy beyond all words; fair spirits seemed
Clamorous and clapping of their hands for joy!
Too happy beyond words, I would have wept
Had I been in the actual world, where tears
Are bred by stranger sympathy; but here,
Where sympathy was life, I did not weep.
Lady and child at once!   I could weep now!
But then the dark hair of thy song fell down,
The eyelid of thy music dropt: it plained
Faintly, and saturated with sweet pain,
Carried my soul into a void grey realm
Of everlasting melancholy.   Maid!
Who mournest for thy lover, hear the lay
And be not comforted, but mourn no more
As you have mourned.   Youth! whose thirsting love

Has conjured an ideal from the land
Of Vision, listen with a joyous hope
And mourn not with the bitterness that thou
Hast mourned.

A louder chord is struck ! let grief at once
Be wept out like a thunder-rain, and pride
Go up triumphant with a purple flush,
And warn of trump—the golden crown doth press
The spirit's forehead who hath conquered all !—
—O Lady, thou art wondrous fair and good !
The earth is filled, oh ! filled with gracious things.
Slowly again to life descends thy strain,
An odour as of rose-leaves seems to fall
Upon me, and a pearly light : behold !
Art thou not as a goddess over me ?
Oh, intermit thy strong-linked power—oh, cease !
And let me drink a silence short and deep,
Then die into the Life that thou dost live.

OUTSIDE THE TEMPLE.

SONNETS.

OUTSIDE THE TEMPLE.

I

BIRTH.

I STOOD before the vail of the Unknown,
   And round me in this life's dim theatre
   Was gathered a whole townsfolk, all astir
With various interludes : I watched alone,
And saw a great hand lift the vail, then shone,
   Descending from the innermost expanse,
   A goddess to whose eyes my heart at once
Flew up with awe and love, a love full-blown.

Naked and white she was, her fire-girt hair
   Eddied on either side her straight high head,
     Swaddled within her arms in lambent flame,
An unborn life, a child-soul, did she bear,
   And laid it on a young wife's breast and fled,
     Yet no one wondered whence the strange gift
       came!

OUTSIDE THE TEMPLE.

II

DEATH.

AGAIN that stage was vacant, that dusk crowd
   Was murmuring as before: again that hand
   Gathered the curtain; I saw rise and stand
Against the inmost blackness like a cloud,
No feature seen, but o'er his brows a proud
   Spiked crown that held the thick mist clothing him,
   A strong imperious creature, tall and slim,
And hateful too, thus hid within that shroud.

Stooping he raised within his long thin arms
   A scared old man and rolled him up, and fled:
And all the crowd shrieked out, and muttering charms,
Threw down their fiddle-bows and merchandise,—
Around the stark corpse knelt with suppliant cries,
   Nor ceased still wondering where was gone—the dead!

OUTSIDE THE TEMPLE.

III

LIFE.

Young men and maidens, darkling, pair by pair,
   Travelled a road cut through an ancient wood :
   It was a twilight in a warm land, good
To dwell in ; the path rose up like a stair,
And yet they never ceased, nor sat down there ;
   Above them shone brief glimpses of blue sky,
   Between the black boughs plumed funereally,
Before them was a faint light, faint but fair.

Onward they walked, onward I with them went,
   Expecting some thrice-welcome home would show
   A hospitable board, and baths and rest ;
But still we looked in vain, all hopes were spent,
   No home appeared ; and still they onward go,
     I too, footweary traveller, toward the West.

OUTSIDE THE TEMPLE.

IV

GAIN AND LOSS.

OFT-TIMES we consummate our fond desires,
   Nor seldom does the strong man seize his prize,
   But ere that day comes expectation dies;
Fruition is not like what Hope inspires,
No more than are the ashes like the fires
   That shed them: when we start upon the road,
   Arcadia blooms somewhere, the blest abode
Of nymphs and perfect men, till, by surprise,
Noon strikes the bell, and all around remains
   The same sad commonplace; nor are we grieved,
Our staff unworn, our scrip with numerous gains
   Refilled,—with Patience, cleansed eyes undeceived,
Silence of heart, meekness to match our fate;
Experience guides us on, but shuts the golden gate.

OUTSIDE THE TEMPLE.

v

LOOKING FORWARD.

How very strangely are these travellers made!
    Happily with no choice but still to live,
Weaving and shaping, so to be arrayed,
    Crying to nature, Stay! to fate, Give, give!
Still hastening towards to-morrow, when to-day
    Fails to bring forth, from its too numerous toils
    And manifold emotions, those great spoils
Wherewith to build a tower of strength and stay
Reaching to heaven. Alas! we only find
    To-morrow like to-day, with the same sky,
    Silent and blue, silent and dark and high;
The only changes, thunder, storm, and wind:
    And round us rise still, darkening all the air,
    Groves we have reared, that only blossoms bear.

OUTSIDE THE TEMPLE.

VI

HOPE DEFERRED.

Courage of heart and hand, Faith first of all:
   Such is the prayer of the perplexèd man,
As the storm-scattered blossoms round him fall,
   And shrinking from the rod and from the ban
Of starless chance. Prayer prompted by desires
   For mastery and godhead sense denies,
And by sky-pointing mediæval spires,
   Symbols of creeds the beaten hound still tries
To shelter under in this pilgrimage,
   Passing from birth to death. But let us hear
What Nature, cruel mother! says so sage,—
   Still listening if perchance gods interfere—
'Gain faith and courage through self-harmony,
And live your lives, nor only live to die.'

OUTSIDE THE TEMPLE.

VII

FAITH.

'Follow Me,' Jesus said; and they uprose,
   Peter and Andrew rose and followed Him,
     Followed Him even to heaven through death most
        grim,
And through a long hard life without repose,
Save in the grand ideal of its close.
   'Take up your cross and come with Me,' He said;
   And the world listens yet through all her dead,
And still would answer had we faith like those.

But who can light again such beacon-fire!
   With gladsome haste and with rejoicing souls—
     How would men gird themselves for the emprise?
Leaving their black boats by the dead lake's mire,
   Leaving their slimy nets by the cold shoals,
     Leaving their old oars, nor once turn their eyes.

OUTSIDE THE TEMPLE.

VIII

AT PRESENT.

But what have we instead? Shelves, miles on miles
   Of books, in all the tongues, from all the years
   Since fabulous Babel's topless tower appears
Through the heroic mist: Museums, piles
Of fragments, dead faiths' and dead learnings' spoils:
   And in the study, victory crowns the hair
   Of our new Hercules, the young, the fair,
Analysis, untired for all his toils.

And what besides? the church bells ring at one
   With custom as respect requires at home;
   Abroad, in cap-and-bells their long ears pent,
Fools go on pilgrimage with knaves; at Rome
A blind, self-styled Infallible, old man,
   Coaxes 'God's mother' with a monument!

OUTSIDE THE TEMPLE.

IX

SELF-DECEPTION.

There's a Seër's peak on Ararat, they say,
   From which we can descry the better world;
   Not that supernal kingdom whence were hurled
The rebel-angels ere Creation's day,
But Eden-garden, Adam's first array,
   Round which the Flood-waves stood back like a wall,
   And whither still are sent the souls of all
The good dead, where the cherubim sing and play.

Dear lovely land we wait for and desire,
   Whence fondly-loved lost faces look back still,
     Waiting for us, so distant and apart;
But from the depth between what mists aspire—
   What wrinkled sea rolls severing hill from hill—
     Vision! 'tis but a reflex of the heart!

OUTSIDE THE TEMPLE.

x

CONTENTMENT IN THE DARK.

We asked not to be born : 'tis not by will
   That we are here beneath the battle-smoke,
Without escape; by good things as by ill,
   By facts and mysteries enchained : no cloak
Of an Elijah, no stairs whereupon
   Angels ascending and descending shine
Over the head here pillowed on a stone,
   Anywhere found ;—so say they who repine.
But each year hath its harvest, every hour
   Some melody, child-laughter, strengthening strife,
For mother Earth still gives her child his dower,
   And loves like doves sit on the boughs of life.

Ought we to have whate'er we want, in sooth?
   To build heaven-reaching towers, find Jacob's stair ;
Alchemists' treasures, everlasting youth,
   Or aught that may not stand our piercing air?

Nay, even these are ours, but only found
   By Poet in those fabulous vales, due east,
Where grows the amaranth in charmèd ground;
   And he it was thenceforth became the Priest,
And raised Jove's altar when the world was young:
   He too it was, in Prophet's vesture stoled,
Spake not but sang until life's roof-tree rung,
   And we who hear him still are crowned with gold.

OUTSIDE THE TEMPLE.

XI

THE UNIVERSE VOID.

Revolving worlds, revolving systems, yea,
   Revolving firmaments, nor there we end :
   Systems of firmaments revolving, send
Our thought across the Infinite astray,
Gasping and lost and terrified, the day
   Of life, the goodly interests of home,
   Shrivelled to nothing; that unbounded dome
Pealing still on, in blind fatality.

No rest is there for our soul's wingèd feet,
   She must return for shelter to her ark—
The body, fair, frail, death-born, incomplete,
   And let her bring this truth back from the dark :
Life is self-centred, man is nature's god ;
Space, time, are but the walls of his abode.

OUTSIDE THE TEMPLE.

XII

SPIRITUAL LONGINGS UNANSWERED.

Self-centred, self-illumined, from our eyes
   Life shines out on the spheres of other lives ;
   Giving, exchanging, filling sweet-celled hives
Of memory ; sense transformed in heavenly wise
And made divine ; do we not formalise
   The Beautiful, the Good, the Just ? and so
   The flower-crowned loves and friendships round us
      grow,
Whose choral voices echo to the skies.

But still the questing beast goes forth, we cry
   Whence came we at the first ? from what soil grew
This endless Reason that aspires so high ?
Where go we ? useless questions these appear,
   For we know nought of that dark sun, the True,
Whose latent heats create our spiritual year.

OUTSIDE THE TEMPLE.

XIII

DEVELOPMENT IN NATURE.

Walled up in sense, we know no general plan:
   Æons long past creative power went on,
   Evolving lights and forces round the throne,
And in the ordered nucleus of the plan
Blossomed and brightened the umbrageous span
    Of this our world, beneath the Fates' fell care,
    The Tree of Life outspreading everywhere,
And seedling fruits from short-lived blooms began.

Have these old mysteries ceased? from fiery steeps,
   From deepening swamps the mute snake writhed along;
Anon the bird screamed—then the furred beast creeps
   Growling; then Adam speaks erect and strong.
Shall there not rise again from Nature's deeps
   One more, whose voice shall be the perfect song?

OUTSIDE THE TEMPLE.

XIV

SCIENCE ABORTIVE.

With what vain speculations do we slake
   The mental thirst! What matter, cycles hence,
   If higher creatures at mankind's expense
Start into life with senses broad awake
To truths we only dream of; hands to shake
   The pillars of the temple we but grope
   Feebly about, who will gain entrance, cope
With the dæmon, and all prison-fetters break?

The churchyard dust a thousand times blown wide
   Would see them, hear them not; the question men
     Ten hundred various creeds and gods have raised
To answer, by Death's door we must abide;
   Blinded by life itself, by fears half-crazed,
     We raise another god and ask again!

OUTSIDE THE TEMPLE.

XV

ONENESS OF ALL.

(PEBBLES IN THE STREAM.)

Upon this rustic bridge on this warm day
   We rest from our too-thoughtful devious walk;
   Over our shadows its melodious talk
The stream continues, while oft-times a stray
Dry leaf drops down where these bright waters play
   In endless eddies, through whose clear brown deep
   The gorgeous pebbles quiver in their sleep;
The stream still flows, but cannot flow away.

Could I but find the words that would reveal
   The unity in multiplicity,
And the profound strange harmony I feel
   With these dead things, God's garments of to-day;
The listener's soul with mine they would anneal,
And make us one within eternity.

OUTSIDE THE TEMPLE.

XVI

A SYMBOL.

At early morn I watched, scarce consciously,
   Through the half-opened casement the high screen
   Of our trees touched now by the bright'ning sheen
Of the ascending sun : the room was grey
And dim, with old things filled this many a day,
   Closing me in, but those thick folds of trees
   Shone in the fresh light, trembled in the breeze :
A shadow crossed them on its arrowy way
   Cast by a flying bird I could not see ;
Then called a voice far off that seemed to say,
   Come, we are here ! Such might or might not be
   What the voice called, but then methought I knew
I was a soul new-born in death's dark clay,
   Awakening to another life more true.

END.

PARTED LOVE.

I

THE PAST.

METHINKS I have passed through some dreadful door,
   Shutting off summer and its sunniest glades
   From a dank waste of marsh and ruinous shades :
And in that sunlit past, one day before
All other days is crimson to the core ;
   That day of days when hand in hand became
   Encircling arms, and with an effluent flame
Of terrible surprise, we knew love's lore.

The rose-red ear that then my hand caressed,
   Those smiles bewildered, that low voice so sweet,
   The truant threads of silk about the brow
Dishevelled, when our burning lips were pressed
   Together, and the temple-pulses beat !
     All gone now—where am I, and where art thou ?

PARTED LOVE.

II

THE PRESENT.

No cypress-wreath nor outward signs of grief;
   But I may cry unto the morn, and flee
   After the god whose back is turned to me,
And touch his wings and plead for some relief;
Draw, it may be, a black shaft from his sheaf :—
   For now I know his quiver harbours those
   Death mixed with his, as the old fable shows,
When he slept heedless on the red rose leaf.
And I may open Memory's chamber-door
To grope my way around its noiseless floor,
   Now that, alas! its windows give no light,
Nor gentle voice invites me any more;
   For she is but a picture faintly bright
   Hung dimly high against the walls of night.

PARTED LOVE.

III

MORNING.

Last night,—it must have been a ghost at best,—
   I did believe the lost one's slumbering head
   Filled the white hollows of the curtained bed,
And happily sank again to sound sweet rest,
As in times past with sleep my nightly guest,
   A guest that left me only when the day
   Showed me a fairer than Euphrosyne,—
Day that now shows me but the unfilled nest.

O night ! thou wert our mother at the first,
   Thy silent chambers are our homes at last ;
   And even now thou art our bath of life.
Come back ! the hot sun makes our lips athirst ;
   Come back ! thy dreams may recreate the past ;
   Come back ! and smooth again this heart's long strife.

PARTED LOVE.

IV

BY THE SEA-SIDE.

Rest here, my heart, nor let us further creep;
  Rest for an hour, I shall again be strong,
  And make for thee another little song:
Rest here, and look down on the tremulous deep
Where sea-weeds like dead mænad's long locks sweep
  Over that dreadful floor of stagnant green,
  Stewed with the bones of lovers that have been,
Nor even yet can scarce be said to sleep.

Beyond that sea, far o'er that wasteful sea,
The sunset she so oft hath seen with me
  Flames up with all the arrogances of gold,
Scarlet and purple, while the west-wind falls
  Upon us with its deadliest winter-cold;—
Shall we slide down? I think the dear one calls!

PARTED LOVE.

v

EVENING.

As in a glass at evening, dusky-grey,
   The faces of those passing through the room
   Seem like ghost-transits thwart reflected gloom,
Thus, darling image ! thou, so long away,
Visitest sometimes my darkening day :
   Other friends come ; the toy of life turns round,
   The glittering beads change with their tinkling sound,
Whilst thou in endless youth sit'st silently.

How vain to call time back, to think these arms
   Again may touch, may shield, those shoulders soft
   And solid, never more my eyes can see :
But yet, perchance—(*speak low*)—beyond all harms,
   I may walk with thee in God's other croft,
     When this world shall the darkling mirror be.

THE OLD · SCOTCH HOUSE
(PENKILL, AYRSHIRE).

THE OLD SCOTCH HOUSE.

I

THE BOWER.

In the old house there is a chamber high,
   Diapered with wind-scattered plane-tree leaves;
   And o'er one corbelled window that receives
The sunrise we've inscribed right daintily,
' Come, O fair Morn, fulfilling prophecy!'
   Over another, western watch doth keep,
   Is writ, ' O Eve, bring thou the nursling Sleep!'
Adorning the old walls as best we may.

For up this bower-stair, in long-vanished years,
   The bridegroom brought his bride and shut the door;
Here, too, closed weary eyes with kindred tears,
   While mourners' feet were hushed upon the floor:
And still it seems these old trees and brown hills
Remember also our past joys and ills.

THE OLD SCOTCH HOUSE.

II

A SPRING MORNING.

VAGUELY at dawn within the temperate clime
   Of glimmering half-sleep, in this chamber high,
   I heard the jackdaws in their loopholes nigh,
Fitfully stir : as yet it scarce was time
Of dawning, but the nestlings' hungry chime
   Awoke me, and the old birds soon had flown ;
   Then was a perfect lull, and I went down
Into deep slumber beneath dreams or rhyme.

But, suddenly renewed, the clamouring grows,
   The callow beaklings clamouring every one,
     The grey-heads had returned with worm and fly ;
I looked up and the room was like a rose,
   Above the hill-top was the brave young sun,
     The world was still as in an ecstasy.

THE OLD SCOTCH HOUSE.

III

MOTTOES.

There is a motto painted on each beam
   That holds the roof-tree up from wall to wall,
   'Neath which we pass the pleasantest hours of all :
And round the cornice is a frieze where teem
Numberless naked children, who, 'twould seem,
   Can do all kinds of work, and, strange to say,
   Can do it all as if it were but play :
These are among the mottoes, Love the theme :—
' Dan Cupid's wisdom keeps pace with his wealth ; '
   Because his wealth is wisdom, says the dear :
     ' Dan Cupid like all gods can disappear ; '
But this was quite effaced one night by stealth :
   ' Dan Cupid flies while Hercules can but run ; '
   And this my lady's damsels call great fun.

THE OLD SCOTCH HOUSE.

IV

BELOW THE OLD HOUSE.

BENEATH those buttressed walls with lichens grey,
   Beneath the slopes of trees whose flickering shade
   Darkens the pools by dun green velvetted,
The stream leaps like a living thing at play,—
In haste it seems; it cannot, cannot stay!
   The great boughs changing there from year to year,
   And the high jackdaw-haunted eves, still hear
The burden of the rivulet—Passing away!

And some time certainly that oak no more
   Will keep the winds in check; his breadth of beam
Will go to rib some ship for some far shore;
   Those quoins and eves will crumble, while that stream
Will still run whispering, whispering night and day,
That over-song of father Time—Passing away!

THE OLD SCOTCH HOUSE.

v

THE MOON.

How often and how vainly do we try
   To paint in words the dying of the day!
   Coming repose ennobling us, the play
Of fretted fire and gold afar and nigh.
This night seen from that western casement high,
   It was so terribly fair with cloudlet-sheaves,
   Amber and ruby burning through the leaves,
I said once more, It must not pass me by!

But when another hour the clock had told,
   I went to look again, and saw framed there,
   By fringing ivy like carved jet, the sky,
The void sky, silver-bright, so vast, so cold,
   The faint moon round as is Eternity,—
I quite forgot the sunset's splendid glare.

THE OLD SCOTCH HOUSE.

VI

THE GARDEN.

THE old house garden grows old-fashioned flowers,
   Sheltered by hedges of the close yew-tree,
   Through which, as Chaucer says, no wight may see;
The sunflowers rise aloft like beacon towers,
Their large discs fringed with flames; and corner
      bowers
   There are of mountain-ash, and the wild rose
   Short-lived, blue star-flowers that at evening close
Spring there; sweet herbs and marigolds in showers;
   Gilly-flowers too, dark crimson and nigh white;
Pied poppies, and the striped grass, differing still
In each long leaf, though children ever will
   Believe in finding two shall match aright.
The paths are edged with box grown broad and high,
At evening sheltering moths of various dye.

THE OLD SCOTCH HOUSE.

VII

IN THE GARDEN.

I

This afterglow of summer wears away:
   Russet and yellowing boughs bend everywhere,
   Languid in noontide, and the rose-trees bear
Buds that will never open; this long day
Hath been so still, so warm, so lucidly
   White, like shadowless days in heaven I ween,
   A moment by God lengthened it hath been,—
As Time shall be no more at last, they say.

Let us sit here! there is no bird to sing;
   Not even the aspen quivers; faintly brown,
The great trees hang around us in a ring;
   Never shall snow or storm again come down,
And never shall we be again footsore,
But live in this enchantment ever more.

THE OLD SCOTCH HOUSE.

VIII

IN THE GARDEN.

II

HAPPINESS sometimes hath a tinge of dread,
  Perfection unconditioned, strange indeed,
  As if at once the green leaf, flower, and seed.
Let the sun shine thus on thy nut-brown head,
So lovely flecked with little shadows, shed
  Through the close trellis as I see it now,
  And on thy neck and on thy thoughtful brow :
Look up, so thought by thought be answerèd.

And let the dead leaves fall whene'er they may,
  Dropping like Danae's gold-shower from on high,
  Rare jewels gathered in thy lap they'll lie :
This day hath been a sacred festa-day,
  We'll lock it fast within our treasure-store,
  And live in its enchantment ever more.

THE OLD SCOTCH HOUSE, PART II.

IX

AUTUMN SUNSHINE.

Now week by week the scattering leaves
    Drift down the sheltered lane,
And week by week the sharp wind grieves
    The tree-tops with the rain.

But clouds to-day have cleared away,
    The sun shines warm and strong
On cot and farm, on hedge and way,—
    'Tis a holiday worth a song.

The air is bland on face and hand,
    Returned the mid-year hath ;
The saddened flowers their hearts expand,
    Simmers the garden-path.

The spotted emperor, seldom seen,
    Is the sunflower's bosom friend ;
The dragon-flies flicker across the sheen,
    Where the yellow flag-leaves bend.

But the shooter is heard upon the hill,
    The robin is by the door,
The curlew cries o'erhead so shrill,
    The swallows are seen no more.

And this is the last last crimson day
    The exhausted sun can send ;
The evening falls, our foot-path way
    Turns homeward towards the end.

THE OLD SCOTCH HOUSE.

x

THE ROBIN'S OCTOBER SONG.

That carol to the cold and misty morn,
   That ending autumn-song, that short-lived song,
   O robin ! I know well, so sharp and strong,
As do those trembling groves already shorn
And yellowing. O brief sweet song ! so lorn
   Of gladness ; all these leaves, from twig to stem,
   Tremble as if dead fingers counted them :
To sing such song men too were surely born.

And this it is : the most desired of Gods
   Is waxen weak, and all his children too,
Even the sun ; that wide-winged spectre flew
   Faster, and now hath caught him by the hair.
Let us contend no more against the rods,
   But sing our last song, and descend the stair.

THE OLD SCOTCH HOUSE.

XI

WINTER COMING.

The strong wind blows from o'er the sea,
    Foam-freckled far and near;
Within the casement closed we say,
    Winter at last is here.

The long boughs of the old trees creak,
    And strike against the rain;
The dead leaves and the little birds
    Are thrown on the window pane.

From room to room the careful dame
    Each bolt and latch doth try;
The storm-sprite on the winding stair
    Sings to her mournfully.

The sound of fast-running waters fills
    The air both night and day,
And mists like ghosts from all the glens
    Rise and are driven away.

WINTER COMING.

Sad is the rushing of railing rain,
   And swollen streams wailing low ;
And the fitful wind, like a slave pursued
   By the fast gathering snow.

From the flower-beds the rank heaps fall
   Across the bordered walk ;
The sunflower props like beggars slant
   In rags of leaves and stalk.

The farmer drives his horses home,
   The cows are in the byre ;
The frost is come, and the ploughman sits
   Idle beside the fire.

Away to the South like the swallows
   We turn our eyes again,
To be lost once more in the labyrinths
   And multitudes of men.

STUDIES FROM NATURE.

SUNDAY MORNING ALONE.

MORNING and noon and evening, week by week
And month by month and year by year, return,
The never-ending harmonies of this world,
Without an end or pause. The mill-stream flows
Continuous; the industrious wheel turns round;
The heavy stones grind on, yet all that flows
Into the watchful hopper-sack's no more
Than needful for each day's void kneading-trough.
The garments cast last night next morn we don,
And still, for gains to spend, our lives burn down,
Until the vintage-time of life's year comes;
For still some guest, unanswered and unbid,
In our soul's prison waits with lidless eyes
Turned we know not wherefore towards the Future.

Here sit I now this bright noonday with hands
And thoughts all free and unclaimed, like some fool
On whom hath fallen good fortune; and behold!
The Conscience questions and almost disowns
Right to this freedom and this idleness.
Why is the wheel still now? it asks,—the stream,

SUNDAY MORNING ALONE.

Why sleeps it locked and limpid in the sun?
For custom's yoke so marks the neck it clothes,
Its absence becomes irksome, and the Law,
Blessed or accursed we say not, seems for man
A thunder-call to Action;—seems indeed,
As much else seems, but is not.   Let us rest,
Now and then rest, and make Time wait on us—
Holily rest, the flowers o' the field and we,
Being again twin-brothers as of old
'Neath Eden's cedar shades.

       This sabbath morn
The wan sun coldly shines, yet fields and roads,
The young math springing through the hard black soil,
The market-cart half shedded, and the stack
Of hay now cut short like the poor man's bread,
Cheerily glisten.   In this small dull room
Steadily beats the red fire, while the dog
Winks listlessly before it; winks and dreams,
And suddenly looks round him like churched boys
Ashamed to nod.   Upon this window-sill
The sparrows light for crumbs laid duly there;
Upon the topmost withy of that hedge,
Leafless and sharp as wire-work, whistling clear,
A half-hour since a blackbird perched: I turned,
Startled by song, too sudden turned!   Within
The village church the household every one
Have shut themselves, and I alone remain
Idle and free.

           The house clock throbs, still throbs,
Heard or unheard it throbs.   'Tween soul and sense,
Peace like Death's angel comes : fresh powers awake,
Freed from the straining tendons of the world.
As one whose master sleeps, may dare to think
Of liberty and thereof sing, this new
Interior life Itself sees without wonder,
And hears its own thoughts whispering thus, 'Behold !
Eternity's sonorous shores, and I
Am here.'   The present is withdrawn, the Real
Is round us inexpressibly : it seems
That the breath ceases and the heart stands still,
Or as in trance we were removed from them,
And thereupon the Soul's white eyes unclose
Upon the sunless ether.

                    Such a glimpse
Of immaterial things men oft-times feel
In silence, mental stillness, nerve-repose,
And conscience undisturbed.   It flows and ebbs,
Ebbs utterly away.   Could we but press
Right through these crypts unlit of Consciousness,
Seek out the sanctum whose ineffable flame
Cannot by mortal eyes be borne, and rend
The sensuous veils that shelter us from God !
Could we but press
The adventure through soul instincts such as these,
Both eye and ear, it might be, would wake up

To an unspeakable energy, and heaven
Open as to the dying !
     But yet why,
Thus hastening sunwards, drop the priceless threads
Our dear earth-born Arachne weaves for us ?
One great tent-curtain all enfolds ; this world
All other worlds, this life all other lives,
Like echoes answer each to each. The stars
Are seen but in the dark, Force hides herself
In the inert on all sides ; nor can we
Breathe but while death conspires ; and only here,
Here where black earth bears heartsease, human eyes
Converse, and passions cling with burning lips,
Dying together ; here where autumn suns
Bronze the bread-yielding sheaves and leaves of trees
Drop to the evening breezes, while the brows
Of the strong reapers melt, or their hands chill,
Bearing the moonlit scythe or sickle home.

All things are types and symbols : earth and heaven
Each other interpenetrate : all creeds
And churches crowning the hill-tops of time,—
Pillars of fire by night, of cloud by day,
Are but attempts to touch the symbolized.

But now the village tongue hath been let loose,
The village church resigns its worshippers :
Staid ancient couples maunder past ; they skirt

The well-known fields by pathways; now and then
Men call and latches clink, and childhood's din
Rings here and there. The winking dog starts up,
And by the door stands with fixed eyes and ears;
Approaching steps are heard; the tingling rain
Of female voices o'er the threshold falls !
--Ah, there you sit; just as, three hours ago,
We left you. The old vicar preached, good soul !
Corinthians, fifteenth, fifty-first, that grand
Wonderful verse—' Behold, a mystery !
We shall not all sleep, we shall all be changed.'
A sparrow had got in; from roof to roof
It flew—oh, fifty times. The quire to-day
Really did well, it did one good to hear,
And like the text the singers sang, ' Behold,
We shall not all sleep, we shall all be changed.'

GREEN CHERRIES.

The season had been late : Spring, lagging long,—
Not like the rosy-cheeked lithe Columbine
We see her pictured, but with frost-filled hair,
And sad scared eyes, had cowered beneath the eaves
From the sharp-biting blasts and drifting rains.
Yet in the heart of nature the great change
Had been effected, and one morn in June
Suddenly all the clouds were carol filled,
Every road dried and freckled with sunshine,
Every flower full-blown, both by hedge and garth,
Every tree heavy. So I said, This day
Is the true May-day, and I straight went forth
The nighest way unto the loneliest fields.
Two hours or so it might be from the town,
Before a thriving friend's well-built gateway,
I found myself, and entered, though I knew
That he would not be there ; unfortunate
Son of dame Fortune he, who sits all day
With wits repressed and sharp pen, gain and loss
His nether lip developing.

                    I swung
The gate and entered. All along the edge
Of the bright gravel fallen lilac blooms
Or young leaf-sheaths were scattered, and small groups
Of coming toadstools showed where showers had lain.
Under the wavering shades of trees I turned,
Skirting the garden's boxwood bordered ways,
Its rhododendrons bursting into flower,
Flaming beneath the sunshine, and at length
Rested upon an orchard arbour seat.

All over bench and table, ground and sward,
The young green cherries lay, yet overhead,
Glittering like beads, they still seemed thick as leaves
Upon the boughs. And young green apples too,
Scattered by prodigal winds, peeped here and there,
Among the clover. Through the black boughs shone
Clouds of a white heat, in the cold blue depths
Poised steadily, and all about them rang
Those songs of skylarks. Other sounds were there :
The click mistimed of hedge-shears ; the brave bee
Passing with trumpet gladness ; and the leaves
Waving against each other. Soon this way
Along the further hedge-tops came the shears ;
Two wielding arms assiduous and a face
The prickly screen disclosed. Far down the line
By slow degrees went shears and arms, while I

Marked the still toppling twigs, until at length
They passed beyond the fruit-trees, and I turned
To other themes.   Above the flowering beds
Of jonquil and chill iris rose the house,—
There is the window of my host's small room,
There Harriet's, vacant now, with casements thrown
Wide open, their white curtains driven about ;—
And see, within that other tightly closed,
The old dame sits intent on stocking wires.
I sat there ; on the seat beside me lay
A cluster of three cherries on one stalk.

   A casual passing picture ! strange it bides
Perennial with me yet !   This little sprig
Of three green cherries, what may it concern
The universal heart ?   Why all along
The road of life do I remember still
The three green cherries there ?

           And yet the eye
Sees only what the mind perceives.   The heart
Hath its supreme perceptions.   We retain
Deepest impressions from most trivial things ;
They are the daily food by which we grow ;
Some future poet shall find fit airs for them
And touch the nerve of life.   For yet shall come
The Poet, such an one as hath not yet
Entered his sickle in those great corn-fields

Whence comes the spiritual bread. Not battle deaths,
Nor mere adventures, nor rank passions moved
By vulgar things shall he sing; nor shall prate
With vague loose phrase of Nature : he shall see
The inexorable step-dame as she is,—
A teacher blind, whose task-work and closed door,
Body and soul, we strive against! O world!
The Poet of the future, welcome him!
When he appears.

    I left my reverie
Within the arbour, threw the green fruit back,
Crossed the scythed lawn and threshold, for the door
Stood hospitably open; none I met,
Nor had I any errand maid or man
Could answer : on the well-known table stood
Bread cut in shives and wine. Then I put off
My hat before this sacrament and ate,
And called aloud that I might even perforce
Be courteous and give thanks; but no one came.
So thence departing, said I, ' Every home
Is thus enchanted justly understood,'
And fared right on for many miles that day,
Picking up thoughts like wild-flowers by the path;
Some of them coarse and prickly, some sweet-breathed,
But none of them were homeward borne save those,
Now half expressed, I have writ here for thee!

YOUTH AND AGE.

Our night repast was ended: quietness
Returned again: the boys were in their books;
The old man slept, and by him slept his dog:
My thoughts were in the dream-land of to-morrow:
A knock is heard, anon the maid brings in
A black-sealed letter that some over-worked
Late messenger leaves.   Each one looks round and
  scans,
But lifts it not, and I at last am told
To read it.   'Died here at his house this day'—
Some well-known name not needful here to print,
Follows at length.   Soon all return again
To their first stillness, but the old man coughs,
And cries, 'Ah, he was always like the grave,
And still he was but young!' while those who stand
On life's green threshold smile within themselves,
Thinking how very old he was to them,
And what long years, what memorable deeds,
Are theirs in prospect!   Little care have they
What old man dies, what child is born, indeed;
Their day is coming, and their sun shall shine!

AN ARTIST'S BIRTHPLACE.

(A CUMBERLAND SKETCH: THE ARTIST WAS BLACKLOCK THE
LANDSCAPE-PAINTER, WHO DIED SHORTLY AFTER.)

THIS is the *stateman's* country: every man
Hath his own steading, his own field, his garth,
And share of common and of moss, wherefrom
He cuts his winter's fuel, building up
The russet stack above his gable thatch.
Look through that straggling unpruned hedge, you'll
    see
One of those sinewy Saxons, such an one,
From sire to son, perhaps, hath till'd that mould,
For these five hundred years; that rough-hewn block
Of timber plays the part of harrow here.

And now we reach the turn I told you of,
Close to our journey's end.   The violets
Are just as thick as ever, and beneath
The rooty sand-bank those white embers show
A gipsy's bivouac has but late been here.
And there is this old village, with its wide
Irregular path, its rattling streamlet bridged

Before each cottage with loose planks or stones,
And all the geese and ducks that have no fear
Of strangers, the wide smith's shop, and the church
Whose grey stone roof is within reach of hand.
A fit place for an artist to be reared;
Not a great Master whose vast unshared toils,
Add to the riches of the world, rebuild
God's house, and clothe with Prophets walls and roof,
Defending cities as a pastime—such
We have not! but the homelier heartier hand
That gives us English landscapes year by year.

  There is his small ancestral home, so gay,
With rosery and green wicket. We last met
In London: I've heard since he had returned
Homeward less sound in health than when he reached
That athlete's theatre, well termed the grave
Of little reputations. Fresh again
Let's hope to find him.

      Thus conversing stept
Two travellers downward. The descending road
Rough with loose pebbles left by floods of late:
Straight through the wicket passed they, and in front
The pent-roofed door stood knocking: all was still:
Through the low parlour window books were seen
Upon the little settle, and some pots
With flowers, a birdcage hung too without song
Close to the window; round them noontide glowed
So gladsomely, the leaves were every one

Glistening and quivering, and the hosts of gnats
Spun in the shadows; but within seemed dark
And dead. A quick light foot is heard, and there,
Before them stood a maiden in the sun
That fell upon her chestnut hair like fire.

How winsome fair she was 'tis hard to tell!
For she was strong and straight, like a young elm,
And without fear, although she halted there
Answering with coy eyes scarce turned to us,
Yet not embarrassed, while she told the tale
Of the sick man. Then felt the strangers free
To look upon her: her tall neck was tinged
With brown and bore her small head easily
Like that of a giraffe; her saffron jupe,
Girt loosely round her long waist, fell in folds
From her high bosom,—but, as hath been said,
How winsome fair she was 'twas hard to tell—
Untaught and strong, and conscious of no charm;
I might describe her from the head succinct,
Even to the high-arched instep of her foot,
And all in vain: the soul sincere, the full
Yet homely harmony she bore with her,
Movèd me like the first sight of the sea,
And made me think of old queens, Guenevere,
Or maid Rowena with her 'waes-hail,' or
Aslauga whom the Sea-king chanced upon,

Keeping her sheep beside Norse waves, the while
She combed her hair out mirror'd in the stream.

The artist was not there to welcome them,
That much was plain; and, more, the life of home
Was not for him; Elspeth, the crazed beldame
O' the village, shouted and sang by sometimes,
And that he could not bear. This and much else,
At the hedge ale-house, while the friends regaled
By the wide chimney where the brown turf burned,
And daylight glinted down, they heard. But still
As of the damsel thought they most, one cried—
'I could have ta'en her head between my hands
And kissed her,—she's so wise and frank and kind,
I'm sure she never would have thought it strange.'

MORNING SLEEP.

Another day hath dawned
Since, hastily and tired, I threw myself
Into the dark lap of advancing sleep.
Meanwhile, through the oblivion of the night
The ponderous world its old course hath fulfilled;
And now the gradual sun begins to throw
Its slanting glory on the heads of trees,
And every bird stirs in its nest revealed,
And shakes its dewy wings.

                        A blessed gift
Unto the weary hath been mine to-night—
Slumber unbroken: now it floats away;
But whether 'twere not best to woo it still,
The head thus comfortably posed, the eyes
In a continual dawning, mingling lights
And darks with vagrant fantasies, one hour,
Yet for another hour? I will not break
The shining woof; I will not rudely leap
Out of this golden atmosphere, through which
I see the forms of immortalities.
Verily, soon enough the labouring day,

With its necessitous unmusical calls,
Will force the indolent conscience into life.

The tiresome moth upon the window-panes
Hath ceased to flap, or traverse with blind whirr
The room's dusk corners; and the leaves without
Vibrate upon their thin stems with the breeze
Toward the light blowing. To an Eastern vale
That light may now be waning, and across
The tall reeds by the Ganges lotus-paved,
Lengthening the shadows of the banyan-tree.
The rice-fields are all silent in the glow,
All silent the deep heaven without a cloud,
Burning like molten gold. A red canoe
Crosses with fan-like paddles and the sound
Of feminine song, freighted with great-eyed maids
Whose zoneless bosoms swell on the rich air;
A lamp is in each hand, each lamp a boat
To take the chance, or sink or swim, such rite
Of love-portent they try, and such may see
Ibis or emu from their cocoa nooks,
What time the granite sentinels that watch
The mouths of cavern-temples hail the first
Faint star, and feel the gradual darkness blend
Their august lineaments; what time Haroun
Perambulated Bagdat, and none knew
He was the Caliph who knocked soberly
By Giafar's hand at their gates, shut betimes;

What time Prince Assad sat on the high hill
'Neath the pomegranate-tree, long wearying
For his lost brother's step;—what time, as now,
Along our English sky, flame-furrows cleave
And break the quiet of the cold blue clouds,
And the first rays look in upon our roofs.
Let the day come or go; there is no let
Or hindrance to the indolent wilfulness
Of fantasy and dream-land. Place and time
And bodily weight are for the wakeful only,
Now they exist not: life is like that cloud,
Floating, poised happily in mid-air, bathed
In a sustaining halo, soft and warm,
Voyaging on, though to no bourne; all heaven
Its own wide home alike; earth far below
Fading still further, further; towers and towns
Smoking with life, its roads with traffic thronged,
And tedious travellers within iron cars;
Its rivers, and its fields with labouring hinds,
To whose raised eyes, as, stretched upon the sward,
They may enjoy some intervals of rest,
That little cloud appears scarce worth a thought.
There is an old and memorable tale
Of some sound sleeper being borne away
By banded faeries in the mottled hour,
Before the cock-crow, through unknown weird woods
And nameless forests, where the boughs and roots
Opened before him, closed behind; thenceforth

A wise man lived he all unchanged by years.
Perchance again these fairies may return,
And evermore shall I remain as now—
A dreamer half awake, a wandering cloud!—
Wandering no more, there are no faeries now;
I hear domestic voices on the stair!

MONODY.

Eternity is silent and serene,
As the illimitable depth of heaven
That presses round the earth on winter nights.
Man comes and goes like the successive clouds

Over the moon, that come from the obscure,
And are found only in the white queen's path,—
One instant seen, then gone for evermore.

He died—but while he lived, some laurelled muse
Was ever his close friend : to me he came
As a disciple, what I could I gave,
But he was richer: honey of the heart
Was ever in his gift, and curious spells
Of richest fantasy were his, and life
Was all before him luminous in its hopes.
  How have they vanished! but few weeks are gone
Since here, at this same hour, his pleasant eyes
Were raised to mine, the while he rhymed again
The verses made that morn : alas! the web
Of gossamer hath drifted with the dew
And disappeared before the fervid noon.
  With sad resolve I looked upon his face
When the white sheet was round him. At his head
His mother placed a light. My tears might well
Excuse hers—heart-sick mother! How those lips
Were shrunk, the nostrils closed, the candid eyes
Shut up within their caves! I knew him not.
It was no more the wild inspired young soul ;—
Draw the sheet gently over him again—
Alas! he is more dreadful than before.
  He is gone truly : some few rhythmic staves,
A broken pen, is all remains of him.

Strange thought comes o'er us when we trace the lines
Writ by a hand that now is dust: we scarce
Believe but that some monstrous trick were played,
And it was not so,—only seemed to be !
    Had he but lived,—oh, had a kind star smiled
Upon his couch and made him well ! But, no ;
'Tis childish to cry thus : the grasshopper
Chirps in the turf, the dew is on the blades,
The worm beneath, the butterfly above,
And the great sun shines brightly all the same,—
We are so little in the sum of things !

Yes, it is better ! penury's pinching hand
Had claimèd, even as it was, his transient span.
'Tis well, for he was born to fight strong foes :
'Tis well, the smoking flax is gone to dust,
The sacrifice is made, the pains are past,—
The white sheet covers him for evermore.

THE DUKE'S FUNERAL.

November 18, 1852.

So, so, now let the great dead quietly
Go to his mighty tomb,—go join the dust
Of better and worse men : give not the dead
What the dead valued not : those cannon-tongues
Speak out more fitly, poets, than do thine.
Leave ye this statesman-soldier unto Time,
Who passes on the night-winds of God's law,
Leaving the heroes stript for history's page,
Cleansing the grave. Your polished lays, 'twould
    seem,
Refreshen no man's throat, and he who lies
Upon that cumbrous wain of bronze, unblessed
By Christian symbol or cartouche of death,
Would but have asked you what you meant, have given
Short audience, and hoped you then would go !
There is false inspiration in the theme,
It puts the lamp out : for myself, I fain
Would have constrained a sonnet ; but not one
Of all the fourteen twigs would bear green leaves,
Much less fair flowers, ripe fruit. Still was he one

THE DUKE'S FUNERAL.

Of England's truest sons, and what he ought
That did he worthily, and with strong will.
By trade a warrior he ; and, like a lord
Of cotton and consols, by wariest games,
Venturing boldly when the market turns,
Never despairing through stark bankruptcy,
Increases on all sides until his name
Is in kings' mouths, and by his bonds are held
The necks of nations, so succeeded he.
Genius beside him seemed a madman ; Truth
Was but contingent, relative to him ;
And heroism but a boyish phrase.
This thing he had to do, and this did he,
Depending both on sword and protocol,
On blood and red-tape. Earth to him was but
Leagues for a march, towns cannon'd walls, and men
So many items to be match'd by others,
Harder, steadier ; both to serve, to die,
For those ordained to rule. To him the priest
And constable were equals ; and our isle—
For he was patriotic—furnished him
Motive at once and commissariat, ruled
His thought and action. Duty was his god,
The Statesman's duty, duty to confirm
The anointed cincture round the brow of kings,
The people in their level, and the plough
Straight in the furrow. Wherefore then should flowers
Be strewn upon his bier, or chant be sung

By poet, requiem or organ-prayer
Be uttered? Let the drums beat and the boom
Of sulphurous cannon o'er the house tops roll:
Let him be lapt in costliest panoply,
Painted all over with new heraldries.
Give him for mourners all those youths who lived
Rejoicing in the smiles of Regent George;
All honourable men, without faith, hope,
Or charity, who generously strewed
The ring and cockpit with unpaid champagne;
All handsome cavaliers, with well-hid sores;—
Give him for mourners all the timorous souls
Who see no providence in coming years;
And give him all the enemies of France;
And those who reverence power; and, more than all,
Erect and foremost in this world-array,
Men of firm hearts and regulated powers,
Who call not unto Hercules, but set
Their sinewy shoulders to the staggering wheels,
And say, 'Thus as we will it shall it be.'

The day was won! proud, jubilant, redeemed,
Their thrones again set firm, as one may hope,
All coached or centaur-wise like men of war,
The princes reappeared: and France, perforce,
Worn out with dear-bought glory, welcomed them,
Lighting her topmost windows. Sluggish Seine
Hissed with the falling stars, night burst a-flame

With sputtering splendour over bridge and quay;
And in the new-gilt Tuileries once again,
Propped on her swollen feet, stood Right Divine.
The sharp thin nostril of the high-born swelled,
The diplomat rewoke all clothed in smiles,
Tuftless attachés like stunned oxen stared
At Hapsburgh, Bourbon, Guelph, and Romanoff;
Europe was saved! Once more, as in old times,
The privileged worthies of the world could follow
Each his vocation,—Metternich trepan
Unwary guests as customers for wine;
Talleyrand titillate his black brain with talk
Of omelets,—good innocent old man.

But these are gone like last year's pantomime,
And Europe is again saved,—France again;
A new Napoleon, its last saviour, sweeps
These old things out like cobwebs, sabreing both
Legitimist and red-republican.
So wags the world, so history fills her stage,
And he who with this mighty pomp beneath
A nation's eyes goes tombward, leaves no mark!

MIDNIGHT.

1832 (revised).

THE lamp within winks yellow and old,
The moon without stares blank and cold,
Chequering all the boarded floor
With frosted squares so chill and hoar,
And dark lines from the casement sent,—
The lamp-light, over the table spent,
Makes every corner of the room
Hide itself in hollow gloom ;
Here and there shapes looming out,
Bench or armour, clothes or mask,
Mannikin in feathered casque,
Like dwarfs and goblins all about,—
Heads and elbows, eyes and wings,
Mere misshapen hints of things.
Close we now our book and lay
Reluctant still the pen away,
Lifting it sometimes again
If any laggard thought constrain ;
Laggard or roving, home too late,
Knocking at the bolted gate.

MIDNIGHT.

Turn the chair and fold the fingers,
Coax the little fire that lingers,
Coax it to a tingling glow,
While the snell wind's northern game
Is played out with the window frame,
And through the key-hole sad and low.
Let's have a cheerier parting word,
Set the flask upon the board,
Get the old kanaster out,
And make the blue whiffs curl about.
Let's try, the day's work ended now,
To see Atlantes from the prow
Of fancy's fearless barque shot far
Beyond the breaker's plash and roar,
Drifting without toil of oar,
Sail or ballast, helm or star.
Watching, lonely, half asleep,
All round us becomes faint and rare,
Like lighted ships in a misty air.
Is that the bleating of far-off sheep?
—Is that a child at the window-pane,
Or merely sighing gusts of rain?
By nature still we fear the dark,
One's own shadow is strange and stark,
And seems to move, though we keep still—
And though we laugh each morning duly,
We know so very little truly,
That we fear against our will!

MIDNIGHT.

I remember long ago
Waking at midnight, when the snow
Was on the ground, and hearing far
Away the sound of a guitar,
And creeping darkly out of bed,
I saw pass in the street below,
Singing a sad song lovely and low,
A lady in red with yard-long hair,
A crown of leaves only on her head,
Splendidly clothed, but her feet were bare.
So passed she singing; I heard her far
Into the night with her small guitar;
And when I crept again to bed
It seemed as if some one had said,—
' That is your Life from street to street,
Passing unheard with shoeless feet,
Over the well-trod snow.'
They tell me, with a smile or stare,
That twenty years can have no care,
Nor can it have a 'long ago.'
But well I know the past alone
Is safely done with, sealed and gone,
And at threescore most certainly
We shall be lighter and more free!

Alack a day! I'm wandering still
By the wells o' Weary, the woods of Will.

MIDNIGHT.

Hand in hand with cheerless themes
Worse than dreams.
So then to bed.   The wind sings loud,
The sharp moon presses against the cloud,
And cuts its through : anon she seems
Set in a ruff, and her great white face
Looks silly and sad from the void blue space ;
Vanward again the cloud-ridge streams,
And we find her out only at intervals,
As a drowning man looks up and calls,
While here and there a star outpeeps,
Cheerily a moment seen,
Anon the wrack drives in between,
And like Time's beard all oversweeps.
To my dying lamp I turn,
Turn I to my chamber door :
The embers now no longer burn,
The casement-chequers have left the floor,
Only my shadow so black and tall,
Steps with me from wall to wall !

THE SEA-SHORE.

Two Pictures.

I. MIST.

MUFFLED and rime-laden, sombre and sad,
    In a limbo 'tween night and day,
As if on an island we stand whose bounds
    Are shadowed and charmed away.

We wander as in some other old world,
    Foot-printing the smooth brown sands,
The snaky weeds shrieking beneath the heel
    That slides from their cellular bands.

Flakes of foam are blown from the ebb,
    White runners along the beach,
Where yesterday's margin of crab's green claws
    And stubble and starfish bleach.

A filmy ship looms now and then
    From the point where the keen winds blow.
Ghostlike it hangs in the air, then fades
    Where the unknown keen winds go.

Wave after wave for ten thousand years
   Has furrowed the brown sand here,
Wave after wave under clouds and stars
   Has cried in the dead shore's ear.

When Jesus was lifted on Calvary,
   And saints long buried arose,
Through the black three hours the waves broke here,
   Continuous as do those!

Overhead shoots a querulous cry,—
   A sea-mew with long white breast
Down on the water sweeps out and away,
   Pursuing its hungry quest.

Old man, what find ye among the black pools?
   Among the sea-hair what gain?
The fisherman lifts up his basket of bait,
   The wind and waves only remain.

II. SUNSHINE.

Through the wide-opened window shines this morn
   The sun with a steady breeze,
The cottage smoke slants and hurries about,
   Golden against the blue seas.

Imperiously the breakers shout,
  Imperiously they call,
With dazzling crests and curved prows,
  Over each other they fall.

The yellow flat glitters beneath the shine
  Like a flooring of priceless ware,
Dimpled and dotted by showers and ridged
  Like a never-ascending stair.

Our shadows outstepping before us go,
  Drawn out by the level disc,
Each wet pebble, opal or ruby or green,
  Casts a shade like an obelisk.

Merrily dancing and leaping alway,
  Hither, and everywhere;
The white young shrimps are merry as bees
  In a clover-field's warm air.

Dogs bark and children's voices ring;
  From the shelving rocks they see,
The sunlit sail of the fisherman's boat
  Bearing home from the generous sea.

From the high house-door peers the dame,
  With her broad hand shading her eyes,
Grimly she smiles as she shoulders her creel,
  And down the rough pathway hies!

REQUIEM.

(Four o'clock morning, 3rd of the month.   David Scott died 5th March, 1849.)

THE winds are wandering through the long night,
Hushing and moaning round chimney and roof;
The ashes fall white from the dull fire-light,
The great shadows dance on the walls aloof,
    While the soul of my brother recédes.

Fitfully crumble the embers away ;
Abroad over all flies the roaring wind ;
And the rain-clouds, through the obscurity,
Hurry along the moon, silently kind,
    Like an opened window in heaven.

The pitiless Norns are visible now
Between the dim gateways of gold and horn ;
For the nimbus of death is over his brow,
And his cunning right hand lies feeble and worn,
    Never again to be strong.

Go back, go back! would the spirit fain say,
To the in-pressing darkness and walls of stone;
For the eye of hope is as wide as day
Through the impending infinity;
His short day's work is but half done,
    And still young the manifold heart.

Come back, come back! doth the world demand;
Come to the harvest, thou sower of seed!
And the kindred labourers on the strand
Of this dear human region plead,
'Go not! of thee we have wondrous need,'
    And hail him with lifted arms.

The black angel hears not; the ages dead
And the ages to come are one family,
Under the All-Father's mantle hid;
Gains, even of art and of poetry,
    Are but chaff from the garner of time.

The blast is wandering through the long night;
Within the dark curtains the straight limbs lie;
Faintly flickers the last fire-light;
But hark, the cock crows! for morning is nigh,
Silently lifting the cold wet sky,
    While the soul of my brother recedes.

BEDE IN THE NINETEENTH CENTURY.

BEING A MONOLOGUE OF THAT INDUSTRIOUS SCHOLAR, RESUSCITATED AT THE CALL OF CARDINAL WISEMAN, IN HIS DISCOURSE ON THE OPENING OF HARTLEPOOL R. C. CHURCH, AUGUST 1851.

I

<small>He hears</small>

<small>the loud</small>

<small>voice of</small>

<small>the</small>

<small>Cardinal,</small>

AH, holy Christ! who calls me now,
Straining the skin back over this brow—
Drawing and cording together the bones
With strings of nerve among sand and stones?
Ah, holy Christ! the cups of joints
Some piercing ichor now anoints;
And, conjured from far parts, I feel,
Working hither like screws of steel,
Fragments of hands and toes. Again
The body of death, with its care and pain,
Receives me, and I strive to rise,
To open ears and open eyes.
I'm no more passive in God's hand,
Lying straight in heaven-land.

Ah, holy Christ! if it be thy law
That I the blind life-senses draw
Again upon me,—the lusts of the flesh,
The lusts of the eye, and the weary mesh
Of cogitating, learning, preaching,—
Shed more unction on my teaching,
Make me diligent; not slow,
Like Alfin, who could hear no crow
Of morning cock, but started up
At the first clang of the cook's tin cup.
Oh, this wretched body of death!
I clutch about me scant of breath;—
That foot still swollen too;—there's no lamp
To find the balsam:—foul and damp
Is all about me; certainly
Shrivelled will all the parchment be.
But from that last dear task I'm free:
Finished the Gospel was, clear writ
In linguam vulgi ere the fit
Came over me, and on the floor
I swooned away—unlatch the door,
Or I shall die outright! Oh, God—
I stand sun-smitten on the sod!
Kyrie eleison!

[marginalia: and thinks himself as he was when he died.]

II

           Where then is Jarrow, where the brave
           Stone church with its belfry o'er the nave?
           Or the cloister all of smooth wrought stone
He looks   Outside?   Some weird hath overthrown
           The land; I'm not myself,—that stream
in vain   Is not the Tyne! the wild Dane's gleam
for old   Of sword and fire must have shone here
           If this be Jarrow, this the dear
Jarrow   Candida casa, with broad roof-fall,
Church.   And two glass windows painted small
           And beautiful.   Alas, for all
           The brethren! for old Ulph who fought
           Hard with the psalter, yet could not
           Learn to read; and Wulf who made
           My bed, good man! and for long years laid
           My needfuls ready for me, so
           That I might all my cares bestow
           On making books.   Alas and woe,
           For all the books! the penitential
           Reading book, missal so essential,
           Singing book, numeral; all gone—
           Bare as a pagan I stand alone!
          This very day may be Easter tide
           And I not know it: let me hide

He thinks I' the grave again, for I have lost .
Count of days, yule, pentecost,—
he is not And fear I am no Christian ghost,
himself till Not Bede, not Bede.
But now I wake: behold the sky
he sees Blue as it ever was; blue, and as high:
And great clouds lying all along the land
the sky Far back, and waves upon the strand
and the Coming and going still. Everywhere
Are life-sounds filling the milk-warm air;
sea, The spider's warps are hung out on each bough,
Clear dew-pools light the hollows of large blades;
Surely the year is ripe to Autumn now,—
An autumn seared o'er with the self-same shades
Once knew I in the body; and the sod
Feels to the foot the same, each clod
Troubling these poor toes torn by flints
And thorns, that oft-times left their prints
Sea-filled on sands or in the marsh frozen black,
Between Wearmouth and Jarrow, hastening back
From Benedict to Ceolfred through the slack.

III

A thousand years, oh Father, in Thy sight
Are as one day, one day without a night:
The outward stream of things for ever flows;
Whatever lived or grew still lives and grows;

The sensuous world still shines as erst it shone,
And I am here to sing the antiphone.
But what is man before Thee and his ways;
Yea, even the sanctuary and the shrine
By which he clings and where-before he prays,
Thereby to find some pass to the divine!
For here I fall back through a yeast of years,
The expected day of Doom through all my tears
I've seen not: Father Peter in the porch
Of God's house nor the penitential scorch
Have blessed me; but I shiver as of old,
Weak and half blind and cold.

The great salt sea doth answer me alone,
Like Tophet against heaven, its undertone
Maintaining evermore against the song
Of earth: the white foam blows along
These unchanged sands. Ah, now I see *and the*
The Tyne-mouth rock, and memory turns to me
Now shall I find out Jarrow, and again *promontory*
Take up the inkhorn and that history *of Tyne-*
Begun long since: how shall I gain
Tidings of all the change gone by *mouth.*
While I have slept?—but patience wears
The hardest stone through, toils and cares
For learning's sake are treasury stairs.
On I fare,—
Utterly new things everywhere.

> Lo! this must be Jerusalem,
> Or Rome whose sacred bulwarks stem
> The Tiber's waves; among the cities this
> Must be the queen o' the world, to kiss
> Whose dust kings come, and I am thought
> Worthy to be miraculously brought
> Across the world to witness it,
> And to record the same. Here, as I sit,
> Long ships come sailing past on wheels,
> Burning internally, with towers that smoke
> Furl out behind them; hundreds of great keels
> Masted and banner'd broad moles choke
> With merchandise untold; among
> Those tall glass-windowed houses throng
> Fair women, each more costly in her gear
> Than Benedict himself, whose mass-cloths dear
> To us from Rome came: on both hands
> Booths with raiments from all strands,
> Perfumes and spices, fruits and luxuries
> Unknown to me, splendours that blind the eyes,
> And make the heart ache with too much. Anon
> Ravishing music from the pavement-stone
> Springs up, but no musician I discern—
> Only a shrine-like hutch dragged by three hounds
> And a man grinding:—wonderous quern,
> From whence such wealth of goodliest sounds
> Are brought so fast! Oh, would our quair
> Had known such help! or is't the snare

He sees Newcastle-on-Tyne and enters the same.

He hears a barrel-organ on the street;

            Of Satan,—ear-delusion, vain
            As goblin-gold whose only gain
            Is a dry leaf?   Now I wander o'er
            A wilderness of smiths, with store
and now   Of reeking furnaces, and cells made bright
              By magic flames from brazen bars as white
he sees
            As sunshine : faces mild, horned hands,
smiths' shops Have these men! Lo, through smoke-clouds black
            Behemoth comes,—alack, alack!
and a
            With red eyes glaring in the gloom,
railway
            And many nostrils snorting spume ;
            Behind it chariots numberless,
train.   Windowed and gilt and bound with brass ;
            Swift as a storm, they pant and blow
            Along their iron way; now slow,—
            And docile they turn round ; they pause,
            And from each chariot's ample jaws
            Wells out a stream of folk.   Can these
            Be children of the 'Cursed one,
            And this the land of Babylon
            Apocalyptic, mirth and ease,
            Gold and fine linen, mead and wine,
            The only goods?   I see no sign
            Of faithful souls, of holy shrine,
            Of learning, the priest's divining rod,
            And yet the folk seem blessed by God.

            But I am wrong! right fortunate
            Hath been my sleep so long and late,

And now my waking when the land
Seems filled with power, when soul and hand
Work equally, when God's ferule
Seems placed within man's grasp, to school
All nature, and with chains anneal'd
By knowledge bind the world.——Around,

He enters From pillared vault unto the ground,
Treasuries of fair books arise
the North Before these greedy grave-cleansed eyes.
Books great and small, an ampler host
of Than pope or patriarch could boast
England In the old time when Jarrow wall
Rose as we thought so fair and tall,
Literary And I, while daylight lasted, wore
Society's These fingers, adding to our store
Some five or six. Sure now I see
library, Learning, the priest's divining rod,
and Hath done the work, and, under God,
Brought angels down to help and guide,
sees ten Wrought miracles on wind and tide,
thousand Or else by necromantic lore
Man hath multiplied his store,
books. And, now forsaken and alone,
Neither God nor saint doth own.
Learning, the priest's rod no more,
Is the common staff in every hand,—
Evil, the tree of knowledge bore,

And now bears good, by which men stand
Kings over nature.

History

Is here too, sending present day
Back on the past: each ancient scribe
Glozed and sifted by the tribe

He finds Of scholiasts; for the flow of years,
With all their dusty blank arrears,
among Have chang`ed not humanity,
them Nor any law man liveth by.
his own Ah, now I see my own poor name,
My own books, saved from out the flame
books That tower and town wreck'd, graven fair,
printed. Fairly and excellently there;
Also Now no transcriber's fingers soil
others The sheepskin or the Latin spoil!
And here I learn what time hath done
about the Since my life ceased before the sun:
modern How the Pagan's steel-scaled arm
ages, Strikes the land with deadly harm;
and about And Cuthbert's corse with weary hand
Translate they to the Irish strand;
history, How soon again the Cross prevails,
controversy And the ship of the Church puts out her sails,
and Gladdening the prosperous centuries:—
But read I right? the people cries
polemics.

Against her; she no more gives alms
Of spiritual love-milk, but with shalms
And pipings drinks the secular wine :—
Read I right? now clerk and lay
Each other in God's name burn and slay,
While o'er those foul fires rises still
A light as of the judgment-day,—
As of God's face behind a hill,
Before which all else wanes away;
' Freedom of faith for every man,
For God alone can bless or ban;
Right of private judgment.' Nay,
Were these not always just? again—
' Reason, this life's law, we'll maintain
To be the law likewise between
Man and his Maker: by the seen
Measure we the unseen '—These
Are terrible words; may Christ appease
Such questions: yet all round I see
The latest still is wisest in all gifts
Experience brings amidst our strife.
Surely the perilous hill of Science lifts
Us up above the ills of life:
Surely by Excellence in my old dim day,
And by its light the Church held sway,
And certes if the clerk fall off
Behind the laic, he becomes a scoff.
Surely God's word is not as ours to hold
One meaning only, soon effete and cold;

But, shining with a heaven-lit flame,
It must illuminate all times the same.

He hears church bells and tries to enter St. Nicholas' Parish Church.

Sweet sounds of bells! oh, dearly loved,—
Reproaching me that I have roved
Into the dangers of strange Liberty,
With duties self-sustained so dread and high.
Let me be guided, goodly sounds of bells!
Back like a child to these green wells
Whereat its mother, its young heart yet calm,
Taught it to drink from hollowed palm.
Saintly sound! I cheerfully,
With all these princely people follow thee
Up those wide stretching steps. Beneath
This carven porch I hold my breath
In wonder less than thankfulness
That I once more my God confess.
The gathered thousands, each and all
Hold our Lord's Book graven small
In their right hands; and all can read!
Let me rejoice that thus the seed
I tried to sow hath borne so well,
Despite the powers of earth and hell.
Each man a clerk, perhaps a priest,—
I enter to the sacred feast—
I strive to enter, strive in vain:
Some hidden girths my limbs restrain!

But the   Ah! Holy Christ, I faint and quail,
As if under the wind of an iron flail.
Cardinal Holy Jesu, he calls again,
calls   Renewing that resurrection pain,
Dispersing my so late-found gain,
him   Yoking me round with a strangling chain,
back. Dragging me to him when I would fain
Rise and press onward: against my will,
As a staff in an old man's hand am I
Thrust about ingloriously,
Perinde cadaver!—recross I the hill,
Back to the sea-shore forced to fly;—
Cardinal, master! there he stands,
With rosy face and large red hands,
Clad all in scarlet!—Woe's me! how
Can I go back to my old cell now!
Man clad in scarlet, who art thou?
The whiff of death comes out of thee,
And the poor ancient childish past
Returns around me like the sea,
Drowning my new brave Life: I'm cast.
Mistily sinking—oh, my God!
Lay me again beneath the sod.

MISCELLANEOUS POEMS.

TO THE SPHINX

(CONSIDERED AS THE SYMBOL OF RELIGIOUS LIBERTY).

I

The silence and the darkness of the night
The busiest day doth follow ; moonless nights

And starless track Time's footsteps; strongest things
Still crumbling back into the caverned past.
But thou, the earliest legend wrought in stone,
The rock-bound riddle of an infant world,
Within that terrible darkness standest still,
Questioning now as then.
I shut my ears to this day's cares, and hear,
Vaguely across the centuries, the clang
Of Coptic hammers round thy half freed limbs:
Slaves with their whip-armed masters see I there;
Thousands like ants; and priests, with noiseless feet,
Passing around them with a serpent-coil;
And kings in crowned hoods, with great sceptres borne
Before them;—red men, and brown-skinned, and swart,
From Nubia or the Isles: what sad resolve,
What fear or inspiration or despair,
Drive on those hordes that know not what they do?

II

Oracular, impassive, open-eyed,—
Open-eyed without vision; answerless,
Yet questioning for life or death, as hath
In later days been fabled,—round thy rest
The scarabee, the snake, the circle-winged,
And other symbols dark were as thy food,

Prepared for thee with cruelest rites and oaths
Of secresy; innumerable gods
Made life about thee slave to death, seared up
Unchangeably, and in the grave wound in
With undivulged negations of all hopes:
So that the dead could only render back
The sense of these dim-shadowed myths and creeds,
That thou wert set to guard. Perhaps the bones
Of Cheops in his firmest of all tombs
Shook to disclose thy password from the dust
And free man's heart by knowing he cannot know,—
Shook when the priests' slow steps passed evermore
Bearing another Pharaoh home,
With baseless rites and fantasies of faiths,
Devised like clashing symbols and loud drums
To drown the victim's shrieks.
And did not Cleopatra's eager blood
Throb at the thought of thee,
While her wide purple flaunted in the sun,
And the white smoke of her fine perfumes spread
From Cidnus to the unknown waste where now
Ships pass uniting hemispheres by trade?
And yet, may be, she knew, because a queen,
The riddle of thy birth and of thy watch
Before the temple door. Her feverish brain
Left her no heart except for Anthony.
And then, as now,
The winged seeds of autumn died amidst

The whirling sand-waste. Not beneath thy shade
The sower walked. Joy fled thee, and desire
Passed thee and knelt upon the marble floor:
And still the passionate heart believes, and thou,—
Thou sittest voiceless, without priest or prayer,
As if thou wert self-born.

III

And yet to whom, O Sphinx!
Hast thou not ministered, and dost thou not,
If we interpret rightly those blank eyes?
Beside the Isis-gates, the gates of stone,
Have blood-red heroes and the sons of gods
Uncrowned to thee. Around thy great smooth feet
The hands of wandering Homer may have groped
In his old blindness, while his eloquent lips
Smiled gravely saturnine, as sad high thoughts
Lightened across the hill-tops of his soul.
The lyre of Hermes may have rung to thee,
Before Dodona's leaves shook prophecies
On slumbering votaries; ere the white shafts rose
Fluted on Delphi, or Athenian streets
Had heard the voice of Socrates, nor yet
Was there a Calvary in all the world.

IV

The beacon-fire from Pharos shines to guide
The beaked triremes with Sidon's wares
And wine from Chios, and the Samian earth
Transformed to gold by potters' artful hands:
A while it shines and then the ships and wares
Are changed: anon the stars are left again
The only watchers.   Temples and their shrines
Before the Faith that brooks no rivals fall,
And from the strife the conquering Christian shouts
Against the demons, and the cenobite
Hurries half naked by,
Smiting thee with his crutch and palsied hand.
In the far Thebaid's hermit-warren, weave
Thy straws, blest cenobite ! for thou hast seen
Bread brought to thee by ravens from heaven's
 board,—
Souls carried upwards upon angels' wings ;
And, like the red edge of averted thunder,
Thou hast seen all the demons fall sheer down.
Heaven waits for thee; thy life throbs up in prayer,
Shedding joy-tears into the passion-cup ;
For these old wickednesses passed away—
Alas ! and he too has now passed the same—
And through the deepening sand about thy flanks
Even thou, before the face of heaven,
Appealeth for like burial with thy kin.

V

Crossing the dusky stream
On the chance stepping-stones of time,
Descending the uneven stairs of myths
Into our nature's cavern-gloom,
Nigh breathless we become,
As if the blood fled backward in the veins;
And when we turn again
Into the even sunlight of to-day,
The interests of the present seem no more
Than fool's-play, wind in trees, an even-song;
And all our dear wise generation shrinks
Into small grasshoppers, or clamouring storks
That build frail nests on roofs of kingless towns,
Uncertain as storm-scattered clouds, or leaves
Heaped up as day shrinks coldly in.
Yet art thou not, O Sphinx!
The mere child's bauble that the man disowns
With loftier knowledge, weightier cares?
Ah, no; for evermore
The question comes again
Which nature cannot answer, but which thou,
Watcher by temple-doors,
Thou mightest have solved to entering worshippers,
Making them turn away,
Earthward, not starward, searching for their home.

Inward and not down beyond the tomb,
Nor over Styx for fairer days than ours;
For night is certain on the further shore.
Watch then, O Sphinx! watch on,
Before the temple doors of all the gods.

A DEDICATION.

(On publishing a Poem called 'The Year of the World.')

Those sober morns of spring are gone whose light
Made the leaves golden round the window-sill,
While pleasantly my task advanced from hour
To hour, until the last short page was full.
The kindling influence of the year just then
Had freed the butterfly, and the lightest breeze
Twirled its vacant winter-shell, to me
A sign and symbol, as I fondly deemed.
'Tis pleasant now in fair book-shape to see
What these sweet morns accomplished ; be it small,
Yet still a landmark in life's paths, an alms
Saved from oblivion and an indolent past.
Perhaps within its fabric not one thread
Of gold is woven, and those thoughts that weighed
Upon me as a duty weighs, till speech
And action free the conscience from its claim,
Will be to others uninformed and null :
Perhaps the sheep may bleat, the small dogs bark,
And not one man's voice answer me at all.

So be it : on the waters cast I still
My bread, remembering it hath been to me
The bread of life according to my light,
For one full concord, one just harmony
Between the chords of lyre and heart rebuilds
The temple of the soul.

    A labour still
Of love it hath been. With the name of love
It shall be sanctified, and unto thee,
Hopefullest friend ! do I now send it : thou
Being the Mneme of past wandering years,
And I the hero of mine own romance.
Nor other reasons lack I, it may be,
Although they might not sound so grand and grave.
As this, a gentle critic wilt thou prove :
Or this, if flowers but seldom deck the field,
Thy love shall sow them broadcast.

       But, no more ;
Eros is the great master, and his law
It is we follow. Eros, child and God,
With unshorn tresses that no crown confines,
Teaches us much. This first ; that the great lamp
Of Truth, whose naphtha needs no vestal's care,
Shines not with holier splendours in the crypts
Of book-philosophy and art-arcades,
Wherein th' ambitious arm themselves for fame,

As the Athenian youths girt up their hair
For the gymnasium, then in those dear bowers
Of our humanity where amaranth grows
With darnels, worts, and thistles. I have paused
Oft-times midway in some laborious scheme,
Asking myself the question,—What avails
This strife, acquiring, losing, when to gain
Or lose is non-essential, and but hangs
Upon the outer husks of life? Reply
Hath reached me from beyond our continent;
It was not I who toiled, cast off to-day
Yesterday's motives, stands unchanged the soul
The same as heretofore. Thus have I learned
To throw no dice with fortune; to remain
Spectator more than actor. Truth descends
Without our prayers and labour. Knowledge stands
Apart from throned wisdom. Trivial things
Minister oft like miracles, and reveal
The narrow path for which we've searched in vain
Through sleepless nights and over sloughs and seas.

A RHYME OF THE SUN-DIAL.

THE dial is dark, 'tis but half past-one :
But the crow is abroad, and the day's begun.

The dial is dim, 'tis but half-past two :
Fit the small foot with its neat first shoe.

The light gains fast, it is half-past three :
Now the blossom appears all over the tree.

The gnomon tells it is but half-past four :
Shut upon him the old school-door.

The sun is strong, it is half-past five :
Through this and through that let him hustle
      and strive.

Ha, thunder and rain ! it is half-past six :
Hither and thither, go, wander and fix.

The shadows are sharp, it is half past-seven :
The Titan dares to scale even heaven !

The rain soon dries, it is half-past eight :
Time faster flies, but it is not late !

The sky now is clear, it is half-past nine :
Draw all the threads and make them entwine.

Clearer and calmer, 'tis half-past ten :
Count we the gains ? not yet : try again.

The shadows lengthen, half-past eleven :
He looks back, alas ! let the man be shriven !

The mist falls cold, it is half-past twelve :
Hark, the bell tolls ! up, sexton, and delve !

IN THE VALLEY.

Trusting lambs about the door,
Entering sometimes on the floor;
Timid ewes with simple eyes,
Looking for them in surprise.

With sunny days and busy feet,
Milkmaids' ditties sound so sweet,—
Ditties of contented life,
And love and hopes to be a wife.

Through our valley goes the road
To some prince's grand abode;
A slope of cattle-pasturing green
Rises round, well hedged between.

With fallow fields in spring-time gray,
Past which winds the long highway;
Travellers' heads a mile or more
Are seen descending to our door.

Sometimes the goddess Poverty
Greets us as she wanders by,
And calls the little birds to come
To pick from her thin hand the crumb.

Sometimes Hope, the youngest Grace
Our lord set up in his high place,
Going to seek for work somewhere,
Or get apprenticed to old Care.

Sometimes Faith, with smile secure,
Makes us feel we are not poor,
To entertain such guests as these
Upon our bench beneath the trees.

Sometimes 'tis Charity herself,
Little children all her pelf,
And our loved little ones run out
To welcome hers with play and shout.

Jesus then the white bread bears,
And naked John the water shares
In a white cup to every one
Resting from the mid-day sun.

MAY.

(IN A LONDON LODGING.)

DOUBTLESS now in Wetherel woods
    The white lady-garlic spreads,
And young ferns hold their wise conclaves,
    All nodding their crozier-heads.

There too the last year's bramble sweeps
    The Eden's arrowy swell,
And the cuckoo over the larches dark
    You'll hear if you listen well.

May is with us, and I am pent
    In the city's huge recess,
But prison-bars nor walls of stone
    Can shut out spring's caress.

Over the roofs from the fields far off
    Fresh influences hie,
Shading the hair from the cool forehead,
    Touching it tenderly.

MAY.

Open the window, let the breeze
   About these brown books play,
And, hark ! the caged bird opposite
   Knows well that it is May.

Sing louder yet ! perhaps both thou
   And I enjoy it more
Within this populous wilderness
   Than roaming wild woods o'er.

Oh, welcome now to come and go,
   You early weak-winged bee !
My primrose pots and crocuses
   Are splendid, as you see.

I fear your sturdy hopefulness
   Already hath gone astray;
Or came you here to teach me sing
   A song to suit the day?

Yes, the summer's feast is spread,
   Her wine is poured out free ;—
Mignon ! I could desire no more
   If I but shared with thee !

Where art thou now,—in hawthorn lane ?
   Or housed with some dull guest?
I'll think of thee, and some have said
   Our fancied joys are best.

But while the mavis sings above,
    And the cowslip dots the mead,
If we together heard his song,
    'Twere a pleasanter May indeed!

SONNETS
ON LITERARY SUBJECTS.

ON THE INSCRIPTION, KEATS' TOMBSTONE.

(ENGLISH CEMETERY, ROME.)

COULD we but see the Future ere it comes,
   As gods must see effects in causes hid,—
   How calmly could we wait till we were bid !
Heroes would hear their triumph's far-off drums,
Would see Fame's splendours ere the threads and thrums
   Had formed them in to-morrow's living loom ;
   Would feel the honours round the future tomb,
Across the sunless fosse where life succumbs.

If it were so ! But wiser fates conspire
   That each shall bear his own lamp through the night,
   Showing but short way round its blood-red light,
   And find, by it alone, the herb that springs
Fast by the wells of fathomless desire ;
   And of this healing herb the poet sings.

WORDSWORTH.

(ON READING THE MEMOIRS BY DR. C. WORDSWORTH.)

I.

Too much of 'Tours,' productive more or less ;
   Too much of ' Nature,' meaning thereby hills,
   Trees, hedges, landscapes rich with woods and rills ;
Too little of the dark divine recess
Beneath the white shirt,—nothing of the press
   Of our own age so full of glorious cares,
   And men that call, new lamps for old ! good wares
For potsherds given ! in this book I confess.

   Yet through it evermore appears in sight
A poet travelling homeward who was still
A poet every day, with common tread
Who walked on common shoes up Life's high hill
   Self-center'd, God-directed, till the light
Of this world and the next met round his head.

WORDSWORTH.

II.

CUMBERLAND was the world to him and art
   Was landscape-gardening. Most sententiously
   A truism or a common-place could he
Announce, and by his grave large voice impart
Value thereto. Steered by the simplest heart
   'Tis said he never doubted, but held on
   Bible o'erpowered: in these our days alone
Of all sane men perhaps in learning's mart!

   But he of all men planned his life with care:
Fast by the wells of sadness walked he on
   O'er fortunate meads with chilly flowers made fair,
Till on his right hand and his left were won
   The waving wheatears of a just success;
   A man whose praise rejoice we to express!

WORDSWORTH.

III.

EACH medal hath its reverse; every day
  Its cloud; each house its skeleton; so here,
  Sum up this philosophic poet's year,
And we shall find within his mental way,
Few threads of vital poet-wisdom stray.
  Instead; philanthropy with hand withheld,
  A caution selfward turned, the muse compell'd
To chew the cud, to sift the sand and clay
Left by chance hill-winds, lest some grains of gold
  Without assiduous sieve might there be lost.
A bald soul awkward with his lyre, both cold
  And over-anxious, find we to our cost:
And this the moral of the whole; *that* man
Is great who simply doth the best he can.

TO THE ARTISTS CALLED P. R. B.

(1851.)

I THANK you, brethren in Sincerity,—
   One who, within the temperate climes of Art,
   From the charmed circle humbly stands apart,
Scornfully also, with a listless eye
Watching old marionettes' vitality;
   For you have shown, with youth's brave confidence,
   The honesty of true speech and the sense
Uniting life with 'nature,' earth with sky.

In faithful hearts Art strikes its roots far down,
   And bears both flower and fruit with seeded core;
   When Truth dies out, the fruit appears no more,
But the flower hides a worm within its crown.
   God-speed you onward! once again our way
   Shall be made odorous with fresh flowers of May.

ON CERTAIN CRITICS AT THE BEGINNING OF THE CENTURY.

THE poet lives indeed. Within the schools
   He may or may not have tried on his arms,
   Or learnt their dext'rous use: but free of harms
He must have dived and braved the whirling pools
Of his own heart, and o'er the heads of fools
   And unbelievers, teachers, priests, tipstaves,
   Or censors, held his own, breasting the waves
Of martyrdom, smiling like one who rules.

And here's the poet's judge! whose learned speech
   Of tropes and classics, fixed authorities,
Smells stale, whose outside confidences teach
   His fellow-philistines to dogmatise,
   Till vulgar scoffers even invade the skies—
Turn, poet! lift thy foot against his breech.

THE EPITAPH OF HUBERT VAN EYCK.

(CARVED ON THE SHIELD HELD BY A MARBLE SKELETON,
CATHEDRAL OF ST. BAVON, GHENT.)

WHOE'ER thou art who walkest overhead,
Behold thyself in stone : for I yestreen
Was seemly and alert like thee : now dead,
Nailed up and earthed, and for the last time green,
The first spring greenness and the last decay,
Am hidden here for ever from the day.
I, Hubert Van Eyck, whom all Bruges hailed
Worthy of lauds, am now with worms engrailed.
My soul with many pangs by God constrained
Fled in September when the corn is wained,
Just fourteen hundred years and twenty-six
Since Christ Himself was our first crucifix.
Lovers of Art, pray for me that I gain
God's grace, nor find I've worked and lived in vain.

FRAGMENT OF A SONNET BY RAPHAEL.

(FOUND WRITTEN ON THE BACK OF A SKETCH.)

'As Paul when he descended from his trance
Could utter nought of the divine arcane,—
So hidden in my heart my joys remain
Lovingly veiled from all unhallowèd chance.
How much I see, how much I do and bear,
Clothing with placid smile the secret pain,
Which I could just as easy change the hair
Upon this brow as render up profane——

. . . . .

Thus far the master, the divine Raphael,
Who died before his brown locks had uncurled,
And left so much,—yet from whose hand we hail
This fragment now across a changing world.
Finish it, reader!—genius, fortune, fame!
Thrice crowned, love's tangled skein remains the same.

THE MUSICIAN.

His sense transcends this world: the Muses' heaven
   Is where his soul was born, a wondrous child;
Instinct above the intellect is given
   To the Musician; wordless, unlearned, wild,
Fancies of heart are his realities,
And over us as o'er base things he flies
Towards absorption in the harmonies
   Of spheres unknown.   Alas, within the maze
Of the actual world, hills, cattle, ships, and town,
Knowledge accumulative, mace and gown,
   Wealth, science, law, he like a blind man strays!
Yet, wondrous child, be nevermore cast down,
   Men hear thy fiddle-bow, and lose their pains,—
   Compared to thee they are but serfs in chains.

TO MY BROTHER,

ON PUBLISHING HIS 'MEMOIR, ETC.'

My brother, latest of so many, passed
   Across the unknown dark sea, where we all
Must follow, as our days and hours are cast:
   I speak to thee, I touch the dreadful pall,
To lay thine own bay-leaves upon thy bier.
   It may be in the arcane truths of God,
Thou still dost feel this touch, dost feel and hear,
   And recognizest still the cold green sod,
Immensely far yet infinitely near!
   Thou who hast shown how much the steadfast soul
     Bears abnegation, how an ideal goal
Robs life, how singleness of heart hopes long,
And how, by suffering sanctified, the song
From the inner shrine becomes more just and strong.

SANDRART'S INSCRIPTION,

ON ALBERT DÜRER'S GRAVE, NÜRNBERG.

Rest here, thou Prince of Painters, thou who wast better than great,
In many arts unequalled in the old time or the late.
Earth thou didst paint and garnish, and now, in thy new abode,
Thou paintest the holy things overhead in the city of God.
And we, as our patron saint, look up to thee ever will,
And crown, with a laurel crown, the dust left here with us still.

OCCASIONAL SONNETS.

PYGMALION.

'MISTRESS of gods and men! I have been thine
   From boy to man, and many a myrtle rod
   Have I made grow upon thy sacred sod,
Nor ever have I passed thy white shafts nine
Without some votive offering for the shrine,
   Carved beryl or chased bloodstone;—aid me now,
   And I will live to fashion for thy brow
Heart-breaking priceless things: oh, make her mine.'

Venus inclined her ear, and through the Stone
   Forthwith slid warmth like spring through sapling-
      stems,
And lo, the eyelid stirred, beneath had grown
   The tremulous light of life, and all the hems
Of her zoned peplos shook—upon his breast,
She sank by two dread gifts at once oppressed.

THE SWAN.

With broad soft breast, with pliant neck and long
   To reach the small fish down among the reeds,
   Hitherward scattering the fresh water-beads
The snowy beauty comes. O fair and strong,
Thou Laïs, queen of pleasure, with my song
   I would enrich thee were it worthier,
   And if it could be but the minister
Of love, that to such goddess should belong.

So I held out to her this page where lay
Some dainty fruits, and flowers, a rare bouquet;—
   Whereat she smote her ample wings abroad,
Raised her black mouth from whence a bruised worm
     fell,
And hissed, as good deeds may be hissed in hell:
   The spray fell over me upon the sod.

SPRING LOVE.

From morn to evening, this day, yesterday,
   We've walked within the garden'd paths of love,
   Till the moon rose the darkening woods above:
We've seen the blossoming apple's crimson spray,
And watched the hiving bees work lustily,
   As if their time was short as it was sweet:
   Along love's meadow-lands too, with glad feet,
We've welcomed all the wild flowers come with May.

Bend thy sweet head; I've strung this long woodbine
   With primroses and cowslips—golden prize
     For golden hair, and flowers that best express
The opening of the year, the mild sunshine,
   And the frank clearness of those trusting eyes,
     Through which there gleams scarce-trusted
         blessedness.

AN ANNIVERSARY.

Madonna! all the year's sweet flowers are dead;
   Christmas is come, and now thou art mine own.
   When first I saw thee in thy girlhood's gown,
Within the myrtle hedge of maidenhood,
Waiting, your frank brow with its auburn snood,
   Like an enchanted tower girt round with fire,
   I thought, ah me! how can I so aspire;—
And now for years our lives as one have sped.

Since then what wild adventures we've essayed;
What jesting comedies our fates have played!
   'Tis now long since I ceased to look on thee
With wonder: that head lies by mine all night;
   Thou art a book read three times o'er to me,
And yet thy last words are quite infinite.

THE MIDNIGHT CITY.

Past these tall houses and closed doors we wind,
   Nor ever any living thing we meet,
   Along each dimly lamp-lit, clean-swept street:
Bolted and barred within, the human kind,
Like Egypt's mummied dead, lie still and blind,
   Stretched out beneath the hands of sleep and night;—
   Will they indeed re-wake with morning's light?
An awful thing this lifeless town I find.

'Tis strange to think too, eons long ago,
   Ere any eyes or any hearts were here,
   These stars shone out the same—unnumbered, clear;
And at this moment where warm breezes blow,
   Filling the sails that left our quays last year,
   The sun lights up another hemisphere!

KISSES.

I.

Within her lips my mistress, then a child,
  Held up a crumb to her caged bird; and I,
  A stripling, very awkwardly stood by,
Lost in presentiment;—was't but a mild
Girl's coquetry, and was my heart beguiled?
  Or was it earnest of the days to be,
  When I too, like that linnet, no more free,
By those dear lips am fed and reconciled?

A crumb of bread sometimes—the bread of life,
  And sometimes but a worthless sugarplum,
    To her new slave those rounded lips present,
Now very gently, then in well-feigned strife;
  Beforehand I can't tell what next may come,
    So I look forward, very well content.

KISSES.

II.

Who can tell why Queen Venus raised the dove
  To be her bird? Why not the statelier swan,
  Seamew or albatross? Our Queen began
In sea sun-smitten, and the wave-foam wove
Her only veil;—What charioteer for Love
  Were better, and what lovelier thing is there
  Than swan full winged, and for the wilder pair,
Do they not triumph tides and storms above?

I think it must have been the turtle's claim
  To the arcane invention of the kiss,
    That taught the Golden Age how first to woo!
But now-a-days we would be much to blame,
  Needing such lessons in love's lore as this;
    So let us hope we are her love-birds too.

THE TRAVELLER LOST.

THAT winding pathway on this windless day,
  With flowering turfs and pebbles here and there ;
  That hawthorn-hedge irregularly bare
And blossoming ; the sky-lark far away ;—
That very twig and leaf and clambering spray :
  And now behind me, from the unseen shore,
  A curlew !— Yes, I have been here before,
And God hath brought me back another way.

One instant ! the memorial sense has flown,
  Leaving all blank as the Atlantic tides
    Fronting Columbus : it was like the moon
To the half awake,—as if I had gone down
  That fabulous well where Truth from mortals hides,
    And, looking up, beheld the stars at noon !

THE NIGHTINGALE UNHEARD.

Is that the much-desired, the wondrous wail
   Of the brown bird by poets loved so long?
   Nay, it is but the thrush's rich clear song
Through the red sunset rung; but down the vale,
Beneath the starlight, never do we fail
   To hear the love-lorn singer: still and dark
   Above our heads the black boughs arch; and, hark!
A wild short note—another—then a trail
Of loud clear song is drawn athwart the glow,
   Filling the formless night with cheerfulness.
   But sure we know that melody full well,—
The dear old blackbird! Let's no further go;
   There's no brown bird;—Ye poets all, confess
   That Fancy only is your Philomel.

IN ROME, A.D. 150.

(FOR A PICTURE.)

FACE against face the New Faith meets the Old:
  The New with its inspiring hopes of life
  Beyond the Agape and all earth-strife,
God-guided through an alien world, with cold
Postponement of the triumph-crown of gold;
  The Old irresolute and faint of heart,
  But loving all sweet things, and flowers, and art,
That deifies nature's fashions manifold.

Sceptre and wreath, they ask for: 'Now, this hour
  Be kind to us, O Gods; let us not dare
    And lose the prize; let the sun shine to-day,
The song be heard!' but gone is all their power;
  Their eyes are dark; a cry is in the air:
    'Awake! arise, arise, and come away!'

COMING AND GOING.

In the bright margin of the salt sea tide,
   Flooding the sands, his tiny shallop tries
   A boy, with new delights in his clear eyes ;
Wading far in and watching it with pride
Tacking, returning, as the wavelets guide ;
   Until the ebb set in unknown to him,
   And then across the seas into the dim
Green waste he saw his little frigate ride !

Will it sail on for ever and a day,
   Or will they hail it from some new strange land?
Why went it from me at the last away ?
He asked, and empty-handed turned to go.
   And often wandering on life's wave-worn strand,
Perplexed, he questions still that ebb and flow.

MY MOTHER.

(ST. LEONARDS, EDINBURGH, 1826.)

I.

A PEBBLED pathway led up to the door
  Where I was born, with holly hedge confined,
  Whose leaves the winter snows oft interlined;
Oft now it seems, because the year before
My sister died, we were together more,
  And from the parlour window every morn
  Looked on that hedge, while mother's face, so worn
With fear of coming ill, bent sweetly o'er.

And when she saw me watching, smile would she,
  And turn away with many things distraught;
    Thus was it manhood took me by surprise,
The sadness of her heart came into me,
  And everything I ever yet have thought
    I learned then from her anxious loving eyes.

MY MOTHER.

(PORTOBELLO, NEAR EDINBURGH, 1851.)

II.

THERE was a gathered stillness in the room,
   Only the breathing of the great sea rose
   From far off, aiding that profound repose,
With regular pulse and pause within the gloom
Of twilight, as if some impending doom
   Was now approaching;—I sat moveless there,
   Watching with tears and thoughts that were like
      prayer,
Till the hour struck,—the thread dropped from the
      loom;
   And the Bark passed in which freed souls are borne.
   The dear stilled face lay there; that sound forlorn
Continued; I rose not, but long sat by:—
   And now my heart oft hears that sad seashore,
When she is in the far-off land, and I
   Wait the dark sail returning yet once more.

1871.

ASSISTANCE DELAYED.

HAD that hand hailed me and that cheerful song,
    Had that good chance befallen me, while the blood
Was juvenescent, and the vista long,
    And life's mid-year unbridged : while yet all-good
Appeared the triumphs to be won, the men
    Who *had* attained, all gods, amidst the mist
Blood-red o'er youth's long sunrise. Doubtless then
    Proudly had I leapt forth and dared the best,
Either with tricks fantastic, or high faith
    And art,—the best that in this right arm lay !
But now the game seems boy's play : keep your breath
    To cool your pottage, wise old proverbs say.
The world still grudgingly unties her store :
Fame and reward are ours when they are prized no
    more.

UNWORTHY AMBITION.

(ON THE PORTRAITS OF LORDS BROUGHAM AND LYNDHURST.)

To rise up step by step from hall to daïs ;
   To take the best seat at the best repast,
   While adulating eyes are toward him cast
By the upstanding hungry ; to have praise
From those he scorns : to see the base hand raise
   The limp hat to him as he hastens by,
   Not deigning to return the courtesy ;
To ride while others tramp the miry ways.

   These are the honours of a hot-breathed world,
These the civilian honours, these the prize
   In church or bar. Behold that wig deep-curled,
The symbol of a long life's toil, those eyes
   Below it like a tipstaff's !—shut thine own,
   And think of Christ or of the sky star-sown !

MUSIC OF THE SPHERES.

(1837; REVISED 1872.)

All things were created by numbers, and again it must be so.
                                                    PLATO.

THE Angel of Death through the dry earth slid,
Like a mole to the Dervish Yan,
Lying beneath the turf six feet,
Till he reached the coffin and smote its lid

With his hammer that wakes the Mosleman;
And whispered thus through board and sheet,
  'Arise, that thy closed eye and ear
    The things that Are may see and hear!'
The Dervish turned him round, and rose
On his knees at the sound of the three dread blows:
He was alive and a man again,
Yet he felt no earth, nor of it thought,
But rose without a strain.

Friends wept aloud for the Dervish Yan,
And a wife she wept for a Christian man,
A long train of mutes had but lately laid
Under the sward in the cool green shade
Of a sanctified wall whose stones divide
The earth where heretic corses hide,
From that set apart for the faithful alone,
And over him carved his name on a stone;
But the dead man laughed as he woke below,
For he rejoiced at wakening so,—
  'I am awake, awake and well;
    Am I myself indeed, and where?—
    Here is no light, here is no air,
    Here is neither heaven nor hell.'
The Angel of Death stooping clasped his hand,
And silenced him, whispering, 'I command
The power whose song shall answer thee,—
As it hath been, so shall it be.'

Beneath the head
When the Jew is dead
Is a clod of quick clay kneaden:
And as the mourners backward go,
Three turfs, green turfs, to the grave they throw,
Saying, 'Thou shalt like these green turfs grow,
May thy soul be buried in Eden.'
Thus in the Levites' vault was laid
A Rabbi, thus were the last rites paid,
At the same time that the Summoner
Made the two Gentile corses stir,
And with a writhe like theirs, his eyes
The Rabbi opening, tried to rise.
'Have the demons power o'er me?' he cries,
Dragging himself with painful toil
From the mould which is the earth-worm's spoil,
And trembled to hear the words 'Follow thou too,
Within the sphere of the melody
That re-createth those who die!'

And thus have these three mortals passed,
Being dead, into the formless vast,
Which we in life, expectant, still
By creeds and myths and fancies, fill
With hopes and fears like life on earth,—
Things for the days 'tween death and birth,
For which we care not any more
Down upon the further shore.

' By what uncertain sense we're led,
  Born thus again—the body dead
  Our mother—the grave our nursing bed !

' Haunted still with hearth and home,
  Hammer in hand, sword, pen, and tome,
  Sun and moon and starry dome.

' Morn till evening toil-in-vain,
  Market loss and market gain,
  Restless sea and wheaten plain.

' Down the darkness go we still,
  Go we without choice of will ;
  From Gentile's scoff and scorner's rail,
  From worm and asp, from kiss and wail ;
  From master's whip, Muezzim's cry,
  Camel and rice, and blank white sky.

' Carried or driven, through sea, through air,
  Carried sheer down by cloud or stair,
  Are we or are we not—whither away ?
  Phantom's of life's fever-day.
  Can we not return again,
  As leaves come after spring-time's rain ?
  The trumpet cannot call the dead,
  Yet I hear it overhead ;
  A madman's sleep is thick and brief ;
  The dawn would give us all relief !—

Ah, 'tis gone, and thou, the dearest!
Thou with moonlike light appearest;
Thou, mine own, beside the hearth,
Assiduous with childish mirth—
Dreams, only dreams! the past doth cry,
In the throes of dissolving memory.
O brother spectres who have come
Out of yourselves,—oh, can ye tell,
Rise we or sink—to heaven or hell?
But even now with my own old eyes
I saw the ghost of myself arise;
And then forthwith I was beguiled
To think myself again a child.
But what, alas! are those below
That to and fro
Pass like men walking fast, and then
Pass the very same again?
Alike they are, even every one,
Not as men beneath the sun;—
Now they stalk our heads above,
Now beneath our feet they move,
Now they pass through us quite, as though
Shadows with like shadows blent,
Shadows from some real things sent,
We their shadows cannot know!
Gone, gone, gone! a fiery wind
Severs the vision, and mountain or flood,
City or temple, or cedar-wood,

Or rock-walls with their multitude
Of caverns void and blind,
Fragments of this baseless world,
About us are flashed out and furled;
And phantoms without number vast,
Interlace the insane dream,
Hurtle together, and never get past:
And a leprous light, a light and breath,
Like the phosphor in the eyes of Death,
Follows each phantom; down they stream,
Wingless, from above descending,
Straight and stiff; nor is the hair
On their rigid shoulders pending
Stirred by any fitful air.
Together they rush now, from near and far,
As if around a central war,
And now in circles whirl, while we—
We cleave the whirlpool steadily.
If any god still hears our wail,
For an hour again
Let us be men,
Or now cease utterly and fail
To know ourselves, to think and be!

  ' Hath our prayer been heard? Ah, no;
   Spectres that have never trod
   Earth with man or heaven with God
   Rise stark and slow;

              Rings of gold
              About their corded locks are rolled,
              Dreadful symbols of dead creeds,
              And dripping brands
              Are in their hands ;—
              Naked giants! how they hold
              By the nostrils monstrous steeds!
              They meet, they rush together : now
              The furies of battle are over all,
              And some struggle upwards in pain, some fall
              Sheer through the seething gulf below ;—
              Allah el Allah, how are we
              In this collapsing death-strife free?
              Oh, that we could dissolve at once
              To nothingness ;—advance,
              Ye barbed giants ! smoke and fire
              Lap us round till we expire,—
              Expire, cease utterly and fail
              To retract ourselves, to think and be!

Thus the dead men from the grave
Wailed as they went ; but who can say
How to paint the unknown way
Within the wondrous door of death ?
Or what the mysteries are that pave
The path to New Life, when the breath
And senses cease to be, as now,
The guardians of our souls ?   The plough

Casts up bones where warriors trod,
Belted, plumed, and iron-shod ;
Those shreds the plough exhumes, I deem,
Little like the warriors seem.

Two lights, two haloed lights appear,
Round like the moon at the fall of the year,
When the sky is mantled o'er
With a fleece of mist, and of all the store
Of stars, not one can penetrate
To the traveller's eye till the night be late.
Two haloes slowly and steadily
Advancing like a double day,
Increasing in beauty more and more ;—
Behold ! they are the tires of light
On the heads of gods, and a golden sound,
Swooning and recreating, wound
From those two haloes, passed right round
The dead men's hearts with a painful might.
Would I could say
Whose voices or whose harps were they,
That had such vital force divine,
Holy Spirit, like to thine !
But what was the song
That bore along
These weary ghosts with a power so strong?
If we could repeat that lay
In the light of upper day,

It might unravel warp and woof
Of this prisoned conscious Life
Tear all sensuous ties aloof;
Of good and ill unwind the strife:
Interweave it with amaranth again,
Die it with nepenthe bloom,
  That we no more knew sin or pain,
Nor feared the darks beyond the tomb!

But what was the song
That bore along
Those dead hearts with a power so strong?
Would I could repeat the lay
In the dull light of this cold day;
Wean the soul from the thirst to know,
By wisdom be as gods, that so
The slave unmanacle his hand,
The ploughshare rest upon the land.

When the sound of the wires
Of those holy lyres
Had the dead men's lives remade,
Did their shadows remain in the world of shade,
Their flesh in the earth
That gave it birth?
Then in what were they arrayed?
But the child just born forgetteth quite
Its ante-natal garments; night

And utter change doth interpose,
And when this life over the body doth close,
And the freed Soul hears without ears the hymn,
Sphere-music of God's cherubim,
And sees the haloed powers below,—
Utterly changeth it also;
And after the new birth again
Forget the ante-natal gain?
We cannot know.

JUVENILE POEMS.

TO THE MEMORY OF PERCY BYSSHE SHELLEY.

(1831.)

> WHERE is Alastor gone,—
> The fairy queen's own latest born,
> Where is he gone?
> Has the far-scenting roe-buck at the time
> Appointed, shed his antlers? does the pride
> Of the wide solitary forests lie
> Moss-overgrown in slimy lizard's nook?
> Has the swift ostrich of the desert lost
> The long limb of her strength, and laid her down
> On the hard earth, which erewhile her feet spurned,
> Where mole and burrowing owl,
> And red-eyed weazel, prowl?
>
> Must he too die like other men,
> Who lived not like them? He who knew no world
> Outside the heart;—
> The spirit whose home was the adytum lit
> By phantasies as by the stars in their
> Blueness of wondrous height; each thought a world

As are the stars, pursuant of its end
Of being; speculating, working, strong,
    Having its rayings wrought
    Around its brother thought.

    An earthless garden grew
Around him, aromatic laurel boughs
    Waved twining there :
Flowers of Arcadian nature strengthened there,
Transplanted from the wizard's world of dream,
Yea, the old wizard's wand itself did shoot
Like the high priest's, and gave strange blossoming,
And fruit intoxicating mightily.
And a bright rainbow'd shower fell glitteringly
From the most holy font of his clear soul,
    Upon this gardened plain
    Where Fancy held her reign.

    A shrine was in the midst
Luxuriously bedecked in its own fire,
    As is the sun.
And his heart beat, and his brain whirled, when he
Turned to it; and words leaped forth from his tongue
As its light glorified him, Memnon-like ;
And the words were, as pundit, sanscrit-learned,
Revivifies from times of demi-gods,
Drawn from the deepest wells of consciousness,
The world received not ; but he proudly passed

The world, and carol'd to
Himself as prophets only do.

The goddess of that shrine
No man hath e'er held commune with, nor seen
With mortal eye,
But thou, wild wingless angel, didst not pause,
But entered to the blaze where spirits alone
Can worship; and didst make libations till
Thou wast so purified, men knew thee not.
Would I could trace thy footsteps up the porch
And to the altar there, so that I too
Would sacrifice in ruth
To thee who worshipped TRUTH.

. . . . . .

Few mourners have appeared :
And meet it is ; for he was ever grieved
By others' grief :
Few staves are lifted for the pilgrimage
To follow him ; few of the busy world
Can go up to the realms where he did go ;
Or breathe the atmosphere he breathed ; or cast
The old shell off, and come forth cleansed as he ;
Few, few have striven
To make earth heaven.

Men say that he fell blind
By daring to approach this source of Light ;
That he fell lame

By travelling far in desperate paths : even so—
Yet reverence we not the martyr? None
Are left us like him ; none are left to tune
The cythera, as he did tune it o'er
The white spring flowers on Adonais' grave :
Lone Adonais and Alastor lone !
Their spirits went together ; and their earths
Resolved each to the elements they loved,—
  One to sunshine and storm,
  One flowers and fruits to form.

  Sage follows sage afar ;
Dark lapse of time between, now marked alone
  By their advent.
As star by star arises on the night,
Up through the shades of time past they appear
In lambent haloes burning steadily.
Revolving onward, the eternal wheel
Circles ; and still a shine from these wan flames,
God-kindled, follows on. Another flame,
  Subtle as lightning,
  Is added to the brightening.

  Still poets reappear,
And still the glow doth thicken to the dawn.
  Redness of morn
Gilds our horizon soon ! Alastor, thou
Shalt be our guide into the unknown time ;

And we will bind about thy cenotaph
The laurel and the olive, and the rose,
The poppy and perennial ivy too;
Glow-worms shall glimmer through the dark green
        leaves,
And great sphynx-moths fly round it evermore.
    And when our many chains are burst,
      We'll say, 'Alastor, thou wast first.'

TO THE MEMORY OF JOHN KEATS.

(1832 ; revised.)

Thou dark-haired love-child, passed
Beyond the censer's odour and its dust,
    Enamoured life,
So weak and yet so beautiful thou wert,
A reverential wish doth draw me thus
To rise to thee with measured words, when now
No one regards the poet's quivering string,
Since thine was hushed, who brought the myrtle here
    From perfect Arcadie, whose verse
    Young earth's freshness could rehearse.

Would that my tears were such
As in the wakening morning, from its leaves
    That myrtle drops ;
They might be worthy of thy sodded grave,
And sympathetic strengthening afford
To me, the mourner, bending over it,
Until the modern world is rolled away,
And all the splendours of the earlier time
Come down upon this leaden life of ours,

Through an unfolding sky,
Trembling in melody.

A bier for earth's beloved !
Trees of Dodona's murmuring prophesies,
　　Scatter your leaves,
Strewn on the wintry bareness of the clay !
Let the sharp blanching eddies of the storm
Whirl them around the fossed wall where the dead,
The heretic dead, repose beside the tombs
Of ancient Romans, whose songs knew no blight
Of horrors mediæval, but were filled
With blooms and odours from the golden age :
　　Leaves of the cold last year
　　Cover his wintry bier.

Through the stripped pergola
The wind wails low, the hard soil blackens round
　　The dead flower-stem ;
Sunk in wet weeds foul rottenness consumes
The pleasant things that were, as it must be
When the wheat falls, to be the bread for us ;
And what the thresher leaves the night-wind sweeps :
After the curfew comes the silent hour :
　　Night reigns most dark before
　　Morn's breezes evermore.

No eventide was thine,
But like the young athlete from the bath,

    For one brief hour,
You stood in the arena yet uncrowned,
Doubtful, although beyond all venturers strong ;
Yes, strong to guide Hyperion's coursers round
The love-inscribèd zodiac of all time :
Thou youth, who in the gardens Athenine,
The noblest sage had leant upon with pride,
And called thee Musagætes, and thy lyre
        Wreathed with the bay
        Of the god of day.

    Not thus, not thus, indeed,
The over-crowded noisy stage received
            Thy artful song ;
But now the numerous voices have stilled down,
The stage is filled with actors hailing thee,
Hailing thee all too late : the winter's gone,
The dreadful tears are dried that wet the couch
Of thy farewell ; the flowers, the fruits, have come ;
        The firmament of fame
        Surrounds thee as with flame.

    And why should we lament
The bitterness that marred not—nay, made pure
            And free of fear ?
We do not think the Beautiful was soiled,
The melody made less joyful to his ear ;
And all else is gone past for evermore,

Or hangs about him like a thin dark veil,
Round the great lustrous limbs now deified:
    Suffering is a hymn,
    Sung by the seraphim.

    But not for songs like his,—
A mortal bound to earth by all the ties
    Of subtlest sense,
And art unsatisfied, untamed, and force
Beyond that known by fettered schoolmen's brains:
Stronger than nimblest faun, behold him dance
Before the wine-fed leopards; hear him shout,
Io Iacche! the meridian sun
Browns his bare breast,—dead is he, or but gone
Into the shade to rest his cymballed hands?
    Bacchus hath but shed
    Slumber on his dark eyelid.

    He sleeps, and dreams perchance,—
Still dreams, of kisses from the crescented
    Queen of the stars;
Or of the dolphin-like round waves that froth
About the feet of Aphrodite, still
In wonder at herself born thus so fair;
Or of the dark heart of the forest shade,
Where Pan, retired from gods' or mortals' ken,
    Utters his regular snore
    Day and night evermore.

      Fragrant, and cool, and calm:
Numberless gnats upon the mellowing air
         Of sunset spin,
The old boughs reach up to the darkening heaven,
The nightingale makes paradise of pain,
And fills obscurity with loveliness:
Or, yet again—a green hill whence is seen
The far strand strewn with shells, and barred with
         waves;
Unearthly brightness breaks the clouds—the moon!
      Endymion, sleepest thou?
      Sleep no more now.

      I would some words inurn
Worthy the poet's name to whom I bow,
         Yet none he needs;
Thou, vestal of the night's mid-watch, and thou,
The heralded of Hesperus, ye speak
Of that sweet name, and shall speak on for aye:
For such as love him with the love he gave,
      His cenotaph is raised in Rome,
      But the poet hath no tomb.

From the Picture by Boyd, Penkill

THE INCANTATION OF HERVOR.

(1833.)

At moonrise, Hervor left her couch
Clad and tired and armed, the while
She ceased not muttering magic runes.
The sail was spread, the strenuous oar
Whitened the dark blue waters,

Still she muttered the magic runes;
In one night more they gained the strand,
And she ran forth to the battle-ground
Muttering still the magic runes.

 'Father Angantyr, wake, awake!
 Thine only daughter, Suafa's child,
 Doth charge thee to wake up again,
 And give her the gold-hilted sword
 Forged by the Dwarves for Suafarla!'
Her right fore-finger pointed like a spear
To the corse-kernel'd mound; no voice replied.

 'Ye of the iron shrouds, and shirts of brass,
 Ye of the mast-like lance and glaive,
 From beneath the stones I stir ye,
 From beneath the roots of trees;
 Hervordur, Hiorvardur!
 Hrani, Angantyr! hear!'
She darkened her eyes with her long fair hands,
She listened and listened, no answer came.

 'Are the sons of Angrim wholly dust?
 Are they who gloried in blood now ashes?
 Ha, ha! can none of the strong dead speak?
 Hervordur, Hiorvardur!
 Hrani, Angantyr! hear!'
She thrust her arms abroad, with quivering tongue
She cursed, she cursed them in their rottenness.

' Dust, ashes, worms ! so may ye ever be,
   Dust, ashes, worms ! within your ribs
   May the vermin lodge for ever !
   It shall be so, unless ye hear me,
   And yield up the charmèd sword ! '
Here paused she again, and her eyes were seen
Burning out through the dark brown night.
Slowly a dreadful wailing rose ;
A white light oozed from out the mould,
She seemed to stand i' the salt sea foam :
The turf was rent, and the black earth yawned.

ANGANTYR.

O, daughter Hervor, raker among dead bones,
Speaker unto the sealed-up ears of Death,
Why call'st thou ? wilt thou rush to hell ?
Is sense departed and Odin's gift lost,
That thou art here thus desperately tongued ?
Nor father, nor brother, nor friend,
Did cut the turf for me—
Two men escaped – and one still holds
Tirsing, the sword thou seekest,
Tirsing, the incurable wounder.

HERVOR.

Tell'st thou a lie ! oh father, so may'st thou
For evermore within flame-chains be bound,

If thou deniest me inheritance,
If Tirsing be not given me!

ANGANTYR.

And if so, Hervor, hear!
The dead can prophesy, thy race
One by one by this sword shall bleed!
At one of thy sons, O Hervor!
Men shall point and cry, 'Lo there!
The mother-murderer!' if this sword shakes
Against his thigh, O Hervor!

HERVOR.

Angantyr! never may'st thou frighten me,
I care not what the dead man's voice can tell.
Angantyr, spells are mine, thou shalt not rest
Until that sword be mine also:
I thought thee brave, but I have found thy hall,
And thou dost quail: it is not good to rust
The sword of heroes;—give it forth!

ANGANTYR.

Stalwart in courage, youngling maid,
Who speakest the runes at midnight,
Powerful in herbs; who holdest the spear
Rune-graven, and standest in helmet and shoe,
Before the blackness and brightness of graves,
The brand thou seekest beneath me lies,
Wrapt in fire thou darest not touch.

HERVOR.

Lo ! how I shall wrench it from thee !
I shall hold its edge unhurt ;
The white fire of tombs cannot burn me,
I dread not the white light of death.

ANGANTYR.

Horrible suffering !
Hold thine arm
Away from me :
Perish not yet,
Cover thine eyes
If thou canst not endure it.

HERVOR.

Nothing I see
But what I before knew.

ANGANTYR.

What seest thou now ?

HERVOR.

Father ! strange things !

ANGANTYR.

Now I ask thee again.

HERVOR.

I see a hand, but it is not that
Of mortal living or dead, and a sword

Long and heavy and gold-chased, burning—
Tirsing is mine! thou hast done well!
Greater triumph now is mine
Than if all Norway bowed to me.

ANGANTYR.

Woman, thou dost not understand,
Rash speech is thine, that sword's thy bane,
Even as 'twas king Hialmar's bane
When in my hand it clove him down:
Hold it thou and hoard it well,
But touch not its two charmèd edges.
Farewell, daughter, all my lands,
Men and ships, arms, gold, and gods,
With this devouring sword are thine.

HERVOR.

Well I shall hold it, I shall lift it,
Till all eyes have seen and feared it,
And my unborn sons shall wield it!
I return now to my bold men,
Where the waves vex the rocking helm:
No wish is mine to lie beside ye
In the hall that burns with death;
No joy is mine to wait morn here
Where the adder is fat and strong,
Or keep thy tomb from closing now.
Sleep then, sires of warriors, sleep!

FOUR ACTS OF SAINT CUTHBERT.

FIRST.

SAINT CUTHBERT'S TRIAL OF FAITH.

A FAIR-FACED man our Cuthbert was,
    The fairest ever seen,
His hair was fair and his eyebrow dark,
    And bonny blue his eyen.

His kin were lewd and he was meek,
    So he left them in God's fear,
And at morn he sat at his shealing's yett;
    The sun shone warm and clear.

The sun was high, it was so still
    On hill and stream and wood,
That forthwith he broke into songs
    Of praise to God so good.

The Saints above the firmament
    Said one to another then:
'Hear ye that song from a land so dark
    Of wicked and violent men?'

But Christ Himself above the Saints
    Heard what was said and sung;
'The heart of man is dark,' quoth He,
    'This Cuthbert is but young.'

Therewith a cloud passed o'er the sun
    And a shadow o'er Cuthbert's face;
At once his limbs waxed lax and shrank,
    And blisters rose apace.

The gold hair of his head grew gray,
    His beard grew gray also,
He laid his breviary aside,
    For his hand shook to and fro.

The husbond crossed the stubble-field
    Bringing his daily bread,
But when that leprous face he saw,
    The evil man was glad.

'Ha, Cuthbert, but yestreen a boy,
    So old how canst thou be—
Now know I that thou art no Saint,
    But God doth punish thee.'

The husbond throws his cakes of rye
    Upon the bench and goes,
But as he turned the meekest words
    Of thanks from Cuthbert rose.

The maiden from the hill came next
    With a bunch of flowers so kind;
Her bowl of milk each second night
    Well knew he where to find.

A mountain maid, she was abashed
    A clerk to look upon,
And she would wait at eve till he
    Into his cell was gone,
Then steal within the yett, and lay
    The can upon a stone.

That day she sat upon the knoll,
    And saw him kneeling there;
She deemed it could not Cuthbert be,
    So gray was his brown hair.

Then down with silent feet she came
    And hid behind the trees,
That by his shealing's end grew straight,
    The howf of summer bees.

She looked from out this covert good,
    She saw the change so grim;
But more than ever beautiful
    She thought his evening hymn.

The tears then from her sweet eyes fell,
    To think of his beautië,
More swiftly gone than sorrel flowers,
    More changed than autumn tree.

Now Cuthbert as he rose from prayer,
    He saw the shaking leaves,
And heard the sobs, then asked he,
    'Who is it thus that grieves—
Is it the maiden from the hill
    The alms of milk that leaves?'

With that he passed the shealing's end,
    Among the trees and bent,
But the maiden rose right hastily,
    And away in fear she went.

The good man smiled to see her run,
    Nor murmured he at all,
But read within the holy book
    Until the night 'gan fall;
Then cheerfully for sleep turned round,
    And shut his wicket small.

Thereafter hunger in him rose,
    But none brought cakes of rye,
And sore thirst made him very faint,
    But no herd-maid came nigh:

Upon his knees he stumbled down
    That praying he might die.

'As is his prayer shall be his meed,'
    Said Christ upon his throne;
When lo, he askèd not for strength
    And beauty once his own.

He askèd not the bread and milk
    The neighbours wont to give,
But he gave thanks to God who had
    Measured his time to live.

The brown cloud passed from off the sun
    Now hidden five days and more,
And from his face—he rose therefrom
    More beautiful than before!

FOUR ACTS OF SAINT CUTHBERT.

SECOND.

SAINT CUTHBERT'S PENANCE.

This hield of Melrose wide and tall,
    Whereof we four are freres,
Was at the time established first
    When Cuthbert grew in years.

And so he joined the banded few
    Who left their cares and strife,
With vows eschewing shows and gear,
    To live a cloistered life.

I ween he was more humble than
    The lowliest brother there,
Scarce would he dare to look up to
    The great gilt rood at prayer

Scarce would he take his turn to read
    Aloud at the midday meal,
Although he was so learnèd,—
    He would the same conceal.

Scarce would he speak with fewest words
    Of Jesu's love and dole,
But ever and anon the tears
    Over his eyelids stole.

The man whom Jesu died to bless
    He sometimes looked like too,
But then his gladness suddenly
    To woful sadness grew.

Oft would he scan from day to day
    Saint Chrysostom's great book,
And all this watching·time no food
    Within his lips he took.

Oft by the night, the winter night,
    When all are fain to cower,
And other monks their rosaries laid
    Aside till matin hour,
He went forth on the crispèd frost
    Right through the snow or shower.

Then gathered some with whisperings
    And twinklings of the eye,
Who went about from cell to cell
    Saint Cuthbert to decry.

But still their spite he noted not,
    So byeward and so meek,
And when that night was deepest dark
    The door was heard to creak.

Then from his pallet suddenly
    A cunning frere arose;
'I'll see,' quoth he, 'where in the mirk
    Our stalwart Cuthbert goes.'

So saying from his couch he slid
    And softly followèd him,
Across the wood into the haugh,
    Led by the snow-marks dim.

Late at sunset the sleet had blown
    Into the eye of day;
Their slow steps verily were cold,
    Imprinted in the clay.

He followed to the river's edge;
    But soon repented he
That ever he did on such a chace.
    With the other freres agree.

For fear came like an icicle
    Into his curdled brain,
And sure he felt the cold more keen
    Than earthly frost or rain.

But from the stars shot arrowy sparks
    As if alone to him;
Till he waxed more wrothful than afraid,
    All woebegone but grim.

Quoth he, 'The youth must have some nook
    Wherein to bait him soon;
I'll find him out although I die
    I' the sedges in a swoon.'

Upon the sand he set his foot,
    He sank up to his thigh,
And further in, hands raised in prayer,
    He saw sweet Cuthbert lie.

And a voice in his ear
    Said clear and low,
'Until my servant press his bier
What thou hast seen let no man hear;
    Thy steps are loosened, go!'

FOUR ACTS OF SAINT CUTHBERT.

THIRD.

SAINT CUTHBERT'S HERMITAGE.

The Saint had grown in years, as I
    Have now by our Father's grace—
When he left the cloister for the cell,
    Alone for a lonelier place.

He travelled without sack or scrip
    As the sun doth day by day,
Till the patient staff he leant upon
    Was chafèd half away.

Nor when he came into a town
    Did he go near the lord,
But with the humblest did he house,
    And sat at the scantest board.

At length upon Norhumber-land,
    Beside the hungering sea,
He stood as the landward breezes brought
    The fisherman home with glee.

'Why stand ye here,' the fisher said,
   'Your eye on the waters gray?'
'I see,' quoth he, 'an island small,
   Afar, like peace, away.'

'An isle of rocks and sand it is,
   And no fresh spring is there,
And in its blackened clefts and holes
   Devils and changelings fare.'

'A hermit's benison be thine,—
   Its name I now would learn;'
'Father, a poor man's thanks are mine,
   The island's name is Ferne.'

Next day upon Ferne's beach he stept
   From the good fisher's bark;
His welcome such as Noah's was
   When he issued from the ark.

The boards of a tangled wreck and boughs
   There stranded by the tide,
Took he for balks to bigg a bower
   Wherein he might abide.

Next, that the waters might not swell
   Upon him in the night,
He made a wall with stones, four men
   Can't shift with all their might.

That done, amidst his earthen floor,
    Beside his pan and wood,
He caused a crystal spring to rise
    By signing of the rood.

With that he worken in the earth
    And sowed his onions there;
And when the crows and sea-mews came,
    They understood his care;

And lifting up their beaks unfed,
    Flew silently away;
Also the mermaids, devils and wraiths,
    They came no more that way.

So Christ doth aid his faithful Saints
    To do such wondrous things,
Their humbleness surpassing far
    The power and force of kings.

Also it is more beautiful
    Than Arthur's painted arms,
Or belle Isonde's long locks of love,
    Or Queen Guenever's charms.

And happy it is beyond the song
    Of minstrelle's gemmèd keys;
Whom knights with guerdons in their hands
    Can purchase as they please.

Roundel and flourish and gleeman's chime !
    Hark ! in the ha' we hear them now,
    The wine is flowing rife I trow,
    This is an Easter gay !
    Saint Cuthbert ! pray ye for us all
    Before we pass away.

King Egfrid from Norhumber-land,
    And Saint Theodore also,
With a silver crosier o'er the waves
    To Cuthbert's island go.

True tears then from his old eyes came,
    (Blest ground whereon they fell !)
For a gyve of love did hold his heart
    To his God-fashioned cell.

' I go,' said he, ' at God's good heste
    Unto high places now,
Would that I might be spared, but all
    At God's good heste should bow.'
With that he humbly bended down,
And so received the mitre-crown.

FOUR ACTS OF SAINT CUTHBERT.

FOURTH.

SAINT CUTHBERT'S DEATH.

My words are few and like the days
   That o'er this brow may flit
Ere you my brethren well-beloved
   See my mass-tapers lit.

Saint Cuthbert knew before they came,
   When death-pains he should dree,
And for the last time took the cup
   Kneeling on naked knee.

Then turned he on the altar-steps
   Amidst the altar's light,
And laid aside his ring and staff,
   And cope so richly dight.

Lastly he doffed his mitre there,
   And every one 'gan weep:
Quickly he blessed them: then went forth
   As a child that goes to sleep.

'Now follow me not,' said he, 'no one
   Must follow me I trow,
Save a brother who can hold the oar,
   I need none other now.'

They kissed his garments' hem and feet,
   They kissed them o'er and o'er,
And many times they stayed him quite
   That they might kiss them more.
But he had caused them all to go
   Before he reached the shore.

And now he seats him in the boat
   With a rower by his side,—
Along the greenery of the sea
   And foam-blossom they glide.

Soon they come to the long black swell
   That heaves their bark about:
Hark, on the naked craigs of Ferne,
   The breakers, how they shout!

Nearer they come, the boatman now
   Holds on to the landing-stone,
Saint Cuthbert riseth from his seat
   And totters out alone.

'Father,' said the boatman, 'now
    The sun dips in the sea,—
Must I return alone, and when
    Shall I come back for thee?'

The west was red, the cold wind blew,
    The clouds were gathering grim,
Twilight was settling into night,
    When Cuthbert answered him:

'Come when it seemeth good to thee,
    Or come no more at all,
But if thou com'st uncowl thy head,
    And bring with thee a pall.'

No more the rower asked, but watched
    The feeble feet go on,
When lo, the door of his ancient hut
    Was opened gently from within.
And an odorous light
Streamed out on the night;
    He entered, and it closed him in;
    The Saint to heaven was gone.

THE DANCE OF DEATH.

CLERK HUBERT lay asleep:
Not in deep sleep, but in the feverish sense
        Midway between
The active living daylight and the world
Of dusk-eyed dreamland, when the memory
Goes dancing with the fancy light of heel,
Singing the while a fitful chant, of things
That may have happened and been long forgot,
Or those whose interest is of yesterday,
        With other things that we
        Mortals can never see.

Clerk Hubert lay asleep:
Not in deep sleep, but in the uncouth life
        Wherein whate'er,
Waking, we have dwelt most upon, comes back
In a new garb and startles us awake,
Or keeps us bound upon the night-mare's back
Until its tale is told and all its train
Of maskers have performed their antic feats.
        Presto! they change; behold
        The maskers turned to gold.

Gold, gold, the much desired,—
And then, God wot, if any one did mark
    The sleeper's face,
They would descry a broad smile flickering there;
For truly pleased, yea, blessed he is to gain
What he had sought so long; he calls his bonds
All in, but when he seeks the heaps to pay,
The gnomes have buried them! Those sinewy gnomes,
Beardless and yellow, and his usurers,
    Threadbare and lank and grim,
    Treble and bass, strike up their hymn.

    At other times right sad
And full of lamentations are these dreams:
    When the lone heart
Is mourner, and before we rest ourselves
As cold night comes, we cast the black weeds off,
And they whose brow was veiled, who have gone hence,
Hold us in talk amidst the loneliness
And darkness: lighting up our lives again
With some familiar action, as of old.
    And the tear doth dry
    In the slumberer's eye.

    By other beds, moth winged
And very gentle, are those sylphs that flit
    'Tween night and morn;
A subtle love-drink do they bring with them;

And the deluded sleeper throws his arms
Into the vacant air and turns again,
Dreaming a hundred love joys in one dream.
'Tis said these baseless fancies can assume
The forms of all things but the sun and moon,
   And stars that give us light
   From other spheres more bright.

   Clerk Hubert lay quite still;
And I would now relate the dream he had,
   If dream it was.
A set of Emblems old he had that day
Been conning, and Hans Holbein's Dance of Death;
And as the eyelid closed upon the sense,
These pictures came again, waxed into life,
And fleetly through the windings of his brain
The morthead apparition junketted,
   And now and then he showed
   His scythe so long and broad,

   And made a staff of it
For leaping to and fro; then would he stop
   A-listening like;
When, if he heard the sound of winsome mirth,
Or children's untired laugh at evensong
Or age's groan,—which mattered not,—he sprang
Alert, and silenced it for ever. Swart
And ugly and albeit wise seemed he,

He neither gibber'd nor did make a moan,
No sound at all he made whate'er he did,
    Hither and there,
    And everywhere.

    And now in the dark night
The minster bell began to jowl eleven,—
    The Christian bell,
With its deep sound o'er slumbering roofs; then up
Death mounted, in the mid-air o'er the spire
The new day was just kissing with the old.
But scarcely had the clock told half its tale,
In at the carven window of the spire
He went, where was the bellman pulling stout,
    By the rope that twisted
    The bell as he listed.

    Then Death put forth his hand,
And at the same time that the man did pull
    He smote the bell,
That split like earthen cup from rim to ring;—
A labourer heard it as he counting lay,
And counting only six, he thought 'twas morn,
And groped about to find the tinder-flint.
Another heard it, a young student, still
Sitting as he had sat since yesterday,
    Scanning and poring,
    Scribing and scoring.

So with a wearied sigh
He laid his cheek upon his hand a while,
  Some strength to gain,
To recommence his task and finish it;
But Death sucked up the oil that stored his lamp,
And, with a moment's dance, the barbèd flame
Went up, and he was in the dark.   Away
Sped Death above the city in a swirl
Of wind, and every chimney rocked, and some
  Fell down and battered
  The street, ruin-scattered.

  Out of sight speeds he on high,
And the clouds burst open, the rain comes down
  As the winds arise
Rattling the hinges of windows and doors;
He is here, is there, is everywhere:
And as he passes the frog turns up
Its white belly, and the strong-limbed trees
Bend to the shivering earth, and pour
Their yellowing leaves like the dust of years,
  And the wavering bat
  On the earth falls flat.

  The everlasting hills
Throw down their rocks at his approach;
  The eagle old
Soars till the lightning sears her wing,

And falls where the blind bat fell before;
He touches the bridge as he onward speeds,
The keystone drops and the great arch falls,
Damming the black triumphant stream,
      As the foam boils up
      Like a poison cup.

      In the cottager's thatch
He boreth a hole for the wolfish wind
      To enter by.
From her storm-strewn nest the small bird flies,
The cottager doth the same, you'll hear
His cry, and you'll hear the thunder growl,
And the rush of the stream, and the forest's roar,
The wheezing catarrh from the chimney-nook
Of the palsy-shaken, and childhood's whine,—
      And each one's breath
      Is sucked by Death.

      Clerk Hubert sweated cold,
As the tempest still more revelled and shook
      His casement loose;
And now it seemed it was the ending hour
Of the old year, and that men kept awake,—
He heard their songs at intervals he thought,—
Waiting upon the bell to toll the twelve,
That they might with their hot drink wish good luck
Of the New Year, as is the custom old;

Again his casement shook, it shattered, and
    Death stretched in
    His hand and his chin.

    Clerk Hubert started up,—
Opening his eyes in wonder he beheld
    The Ancient One.
Men see in sleep,—but whether he still slept,
Or whether 'twas a trance, a charm, that wrought
At that strange instant of eternal time,
When earth and sun combine to start afresh,
And we must add a cypher to our date—
The blood and brain this epoch shares perchance—
Or whether 'twas a restlessness of heart,
I know not, but he started and stood up ;
    For who can answer 'Nay,'
    When Death sayeth 'Yea.'

'Come out, come out with me,
And I will show thee one night's government
    Of my vast realm :
Sceptre and sword and throne I have none, these
I give unto my helpmates : but come thou,
And heaven and hell will be revealed to thee
And all the opening pageants of the grave.
    Come thou with me ;
    I touch thine eyes, they see.

'I am the one whose thought
Is as the deed ; no power before me went,
And none shall come
Behind me ; I am strengthened with the years :
A nether Omega am I : a chain
I bound round all things lasts for evermore :
Under my touch, Man vanishes as doth
The worm he germinates, the moth that comes
From the maggot, the invisible living thing
That stirs upon the moth,—I am inborn
With all lives, and
With all lives I expand.

'But fear me not, I am
The hoary dust, the shut ear, the profound,
The heart at rest,
The tongueless negative of nature's lies,—
Fear me not, for I am the blood that flows
Within thee ; I am change ; it is even I
Creates a joy and triumph when thou feel'st
New powers within thee ; I alone can make
The old give place
To thy onward race.

'All men are born to me ;
I am the father, mother,—yet ye hate
Me foolishly :
An easy spirit and a free lives on,

But he who fears the ice doth stumble ; walk
Peacefully, confidently ; I'm thy friend,
To walk with thee in peace : but grudge and weep
And carp, I'll be a cold chain round thy neck
Into the grave, each day a link drawn in,
Until thy face shall be upon the turf,
  And the hair from thy crown
  Be blown like thistle-down.'

  The speaker without breath
Here ceasèd, and Clerk Hubert winced and groaned,
   Withouten power
To speak the horrors that within him stirred,—
A desperate case was his indeed, till Death
Grew tired of waiting, and took hold of him,
Or nearly did—in vain again he tried
To shout, now mouth to mouth with that dread lord,
  Who stood by the bed,
  Close to his head.

  Such trembling seized his limbs
As shook the stented couch ; whereat the dame
   Who by him lay,
The wedded mistress of this learnèd Clerk,
Woke up in gentle fear for her good lord,
And roused him up and made him tell his dream,
Signing the cross on her brow and his own,

For he averr'd Death next would come to her,
        And that her life
        Would end the strife.

    But this she would not hear,
But rather deemed his love alone had brought
        The phantom there.
He answered, 'Nay, that Death was by them still,
And that her passing-bell was in his ear,
Nor would a few months pass till every man
Would hear it.' Then she soothed him with sweet words,
        Again in a short while
Once more sleep held them in its coil.

    But the morning arose
      On a long sheeted corse,
    And the stable-boy combing
      A coal-black horse:
The corse was Clerk Hubert's;
    The black horse ere long
Drew the bier to the church-vault
    With prayer and song.

A FABLE.

(1832.)

Two striplings in the ancient time
Between themselves agreed to climb
The Holy Mount; perchance they'd see
Something of life's great mystery,
Through the smoke or through the fires
That hill's Tartarean throat respires.
Forthwith they fixed with leathern thong
Their brazen sandals high and strong,
And bent their knees to the ascent
A league or two, when overspent
And breathless, one of them cried out,
'Comrade, hold! I'm not so stout
As thus to urge for long; I'll call
The sun to stay awhile his fall,
And give us time to rest us here!'
So with a self-complacent peer
Adown the slope, he stretched himself
Like one who would give all his pelf
For a snug retreat and a full wine-cup,

And would say to himself, I shall drink it up,
I deserve it all, I have done enough,
Labour without a fee's all stuff!
The other adventurer looked up still,
Scanning and measuring all the hill;
Lost he seem'd in expectation,
Living on hope's immaterial ration;
But now, while nursing his left foot
As if it were sick, cried the first, 'Let's put
A great stone here to mark the spot
Before we start again; why not?'
His comrade half indignant rose
And clipt a snail by its shrinking nose
Between his finger and his thumb,
And with a grand flourish derisive and dumb,
Placed it for the monument,
Then set himself to the ascent.
So now again for an hour or so
Abreast like loving friends they go;
Wading scoria, vaulting creeks
Where the sluggish lava reeks,
When suddenly he who before had stopt,
In a fainting fit of laughter dropt.
'Ha! my comrade bold,' quoth he,
'I have been thinking, ha, ha, he!
I have been thinking, that a cat,
Or a squirrel, a weasel, or even a rat,
Could climb this hill much better than we!

What fools we are one drop of sweat
To lose in such a monstrous fret,
Making a toil of a pleasure.   No!
Let's lie down here an hour or so,
Until the sun gets round the hill.'
'Nay!' cries his companion, 'if you will
Rest here, you shall rest alone, not I,
And long enough before you spy
The top, I'm there.'   With that he left
The weak one seeking a shady cleft.

Onward sped he through the glare,
With naked breast and loosened hair;
Onward still he won his way
And touched the sky ere close of day.

Next morn a rabble with horn-books, beads,
Bells, drums, masks, and other small needs
For mumming and make-believe, descried
The laggard slumbering on his side.
He was not half-way up the hill,
And yet a great way above them still;
Something they wanted to gabble about,
And there was he! so they raised a shout,
Wonderful!—a mere boy! oh,
Such love of science and such a flow
Of perseverance, courage, all
Supposable virtues great and small!

Doubtless he hath toiled all night
Without either supper or lantern-light,
And now returns in time to greet
Our wise-heads with the hill's last feat.
Mighty traveller! They shout,
Till he starts and wakes and looks about,
Rubbing his eyes and wondering why
They stare at him so, stare and cry,
Mighty traveller! But soon
He saw it was indeed full moon,
Full tide I rather ought to say
For him and his affairs that day.
—'Tis true he had been outstripped far,
But why should that be the smallest bar;
His comrade, the true conqueror, he
Is just too high for them to see,—
Down steps Sir Magnanimity
With air coquettish, pleased and shy,
The mummers raise him shoulder high,
And with their awkward backs round bent,
The youth of genius smiles content.
On to the temple where all stuff
Useless elsewhere shares the puff
Of incense now they carry him,
With damnable clatter and chant of hymn;
Cobbler, patcher, quidnunc, drone,
'Idea-less girl,' and long-tongued crone,
Running together, a quack never lacks

Bolstering from bolstered quacks,
'Claw me—claw thee,' suits both the backs!
But it is, good sooth, a stint of labour
To dance and leap, with pipe and tabor
Stunning the wide-mouthed beholders,
With a false god on one's shoulders;
So they seat him on the shrine
And aver he looks divine,
Although at first he feels but queer,
And now and then begins to fear
His honours may be overdone,
Even if he be Apollo's son;
When lo, like Moses from Sinai,
The other traveller stands close by!
He had seen the moon's eclipse
Through the fire from Etna's lips,
With Orion had he spoken,
His fast with honey-dew had broken,
Seen the nether world unveiled,
Nor had fainted nor had quailed:
And here he stands amidst the throng,
On his tongue a wise sweet song,
In his hand a laurel fair,
An opal rainbow round his hair,
Truth reigning from his great mild eye,
And in his heart humility.
Cease their din the rabble-rout,
And mutter and whisper all about,

'What's his name, and whence comes he?
What may here his business be?
Do you understand his speech?
He seems at once to sing and preach!'
The cobblers, patchers, quidnuncs, drones,
'Idea-less girls' and long-tongued crones,
Nod and wink and say, 'So, so,
We've chosen our Genius, and want no mo',
One like ourselves we've chosen, one
Who has not with such haste begun,
One who can sing and who can preach,
Who can whistle as well as teach,
But one who is not such a dunce
As to addle our heads by them all at once!'
With that they drive him from the place,
They raise their hands against his face,
They will not suffer his eyes' sharp light,
They mock him and drive him into night.
O saddest sight of all, they steal
The laurel when his senses reel,
And give it to their favourite!

But whether the history endeth here,
Doth not certainly appear:
Time bears a wallet at his back,
And very willingly 'gives the sack'

To much that glitters proud and fine;
While the shoots that nature loves ne'er tine,
But grow and grow, and the birds of the air
Find nourishment and harbour there.

DEDICATIO POSTICA.

Now many years ago in life's midday,
   I laid the pen aside and rested still,
   Like one barefooted on a shingly hill:
Three poets then came past, each young as May,
Year after year, upon their upward way,
   And each one reached his hand out as he passed,
   And over me his friendship's mantle cast,
And went on singing, everyone his lay.
Which was the earliest? methinks 'twas he
   Who from the Southern laurels fresh leaves brought,
     Then he who from the North learned Scaldic power,
   And last the youngest, with the rainbow wrought
     About his head; a symbol and a dower.—
But I can't choose between these brethren three.

LONDON : PRINTED BY
SPOTTISWOODE AND CO., NEW-STREET SQUARE
AND PARLIAMENT STREET

www.ingramcontent.com/pod-product-compliance
Lightning Source LLC
Chambersburg PA
CBHW031341230426
43670CB00006B/404